Tell Me About Yourself

Storytelling to Get Jobs and Propel Your Career

by Katharine Hansen, Ph.D.

Tell Me About Yourself

Published by JIST Works, an imprint of JIST Publishing
7321 Shadeland Station, Suite 200
Indianapolis, IN 46256

Phone: 800-648-JIST Fax: 877-454-7839 E-mail: info@jist.com

Visit our Web site at **www.jist.com** for information on JIST, free job search tips, tables of contents and sample pages, and ordering instructions for our many products!

Trade Product Manager: Lori Cates Hand
Cover Designer: Honeymoon Image & Design, Inc.
Interior Designer: Aleata Halbig
Proofreaders: Chuck Hutchinson, Jeanne Clark
Indexer: Kelly D. Henthorne

Printed in the United States of America
14 13 12 11 10 09 9 8 7 6 5 4 3 2

Library of Congress Cataloging-in-Publication Data
Hansen, Katharine.
Tell me about yourself : storytelling to get jobs and propel your career / by Katharine Hansen.
p. cm.
Includes index.
ISBN 978-1-59357-670-7 (alk. paper)
1. Employment interviewing. 2. Storytelling. I. Title.
HF5549.5.I6H346 2009
650.14'4--dc22

2009003671

ISBN 978-1-59357-670-7

Dedication

This book is dedicated to the memory of Kevin Sharpe, Ph.D., my core faculty advisor during my doctoral program, who oversaw my work on both this book and its companion dissertation. I am grateful that my story intersected with Kevin's, if only for a brief period.

CONTENTS

Acknowledgments

Many people have contributed to this book and my doctoral dissertation research. I'd like to thank Dr. Robert Boozer, through whose class I discovered organizational storytelling. I thank Cynthia M. Buenger and John R. Hansen for their invaluable research assistance. I thank my research participants and students for telling their stories. Many thanks to Deb Wile Dib, Roberta Gamza, Norine Dagliano, Meg Guiseppi, and other members of the Career Management Alliance, who shared their insights and samples. Thanks to Robert S. Frey and Lori Silverman for their excellent information. I owe a huge debt of gratitude to Dr. Bobbi Kerlin for her methodology guidance. I'm grateful to the "pioneers" of business storytelling such as Steve Denning, Annette Simmons, Terence Gargiulo, and many others. Thank you to Dr. Jane Johansen for editorial tutelage. Much appreciation to Dr. Monique Forte for her mentoring. I greatly appreciate the support of my doctoral committee, the late Dr. Kevin Sharpe, Dr. Sherry Eve Penn, Dr. Rebecca J. Oliphant, Dr. Cindy Lovell Oliver, Dr. Cheryl A. Lossie, Dr. Alison Nordström, Dr. Elizabeth Weir Weatherly, and former committee member Dr. Sandra Hurlong. I also thank all the faculty, staff, and administration at Union Institute & University who have supported my work as well as supporters at Stetson University, especially Dr. Paul Dascher and Dr. Roberta Favis. I appreciate the research support provided by the Business School Foundation and Dr. Judson Stryker at Stetson. I thank the 11 members of the Resiliency Colloquium, especially Anne Bedwinek and Becky Ridge, for being there for me. Thanks to Lori Cates Hand and the folks at JIST for a painless editing process. Thanks and love to my sister, Carolynn Hood, for her contributions, and to Brett Bayne, my friend for more than 25 years.

Most of all, I thank Dr. Randall S. Hansen for his writing contributions, editorial guidance, critiques, unfailing support, endorphin-producing bike rides, partnership, and love.

Why Use Storytelling in Your Job Search?

Once upon a time, a job seeker underwent a frustrating series of interviews over a five-month period with no job offer. Then the discouraged young man read a book that suggested composing personal stories. Doing so, the job seeker found, provided him with better interview preparation than any coaching he had ever experienced. Using stories he hadn't remembered before he read the book, he said, made him more confident, convincing, and persuasive in his interviews. Stories enabled him to present himself in a personable and powerful way to his interviewers. He again used stories during the next round of interviews. The tale ends happily with his hiring in an executive position that represented a major advance in his career. The job seeker in this story is a real person who posted a review on Amazon.com of Annette Simmons's 2006 book, *The Story Factor.*

Tell Me About Yourself: Storytelling to Get Jobs and Propel Your Career extends the ideas of Simmons and other current authors who tout the value of storytelling. The volume you hold in your hands focuses on a narrow yet powerful use of storytelling: telling stories to advance your career, whether by moving up in your current organization or landing a job in a new organization. The title comes from the most commonly asked question (which isn't even a question but a request) in job interviews: "Tell me about yourself." Composing stories to reveal your personal and professional self in response to that "question" is just one way to use storytelling to propel your career.

Simmons writes that the natural reaction of an unfamiliar person whom you hope to influence is to distrust you—until you answer two major questions. The first question is "Who are you?" In resumes, cover letters, portfolios, and interviews, job seekers attempt to tell who they are, but how often do you think these communications really convey a sense of who the job seeker is? Simmons's second question, "Why are you here?" can be translated as "Why are you contacting this employer?" "Why are you interviewing for a job here?" and "Why do you want to work for this organization?"

How Storytelling Can Help You Get a Job

But answering those questions is just the beginning of how storytelling can springboard your job search and career advancement. Here are more reasons that storytelling is especially appropriate in the job hunt.

Stories Establish Your Identity and Reveal Your Personality

Stories satisfy the basic human need to be known. Clearly, being known among employers is a major goal of job seekers, and it is in large part through resumes, cover letters, portfolios, and employment interviews that employers get to know candidates. Job seekers can gain the employer's recognition by integrating storytelling into these career-marketing communications.

In *Training & Development* magazine, Bonnie Durrance tells a tale that exemplifies the notion of revealing one's personality through story. She describes an aspiring dancer exuding happiness and a positive attitude while collecting tolls in a tollbooth. Whereas many toll-takers might consider such a job soul deadening, the protagonist in Durrance's story radiates joy because he turns on music and practices his true aspiration—dancing—in his tollbooth throughout his shift. "We can feel the story move us," Durrance writes, "opening windows of possibilities, expanding our idea of work, and challenging our thoughts about jobs, dreams, and tollbooths." It's not difficult to picture the toll-taker/dancer interviewing for his next job and dazzling the interviewer with his upbeat take on making the best of a dull job.

Stories Help You Know Yourself and Build Confidence

Not only can telling stories enable others to know you better; they can also help you get to know yourself better. Developing and telling your stories can become the underpinning for self-authentication. As you see common threads and patterns emerging in your stories, you'll understand more about yourself, your goals, your best career path, and your ideal job—and this understanding can't help but boost your confidence and improve your ability to sell yourself to an employer.

An emerging movement in career counseling involves constructing career narratives that enable job seekers to uncover meaning and connections. They become central characters in their own stories and plot their own futures.

Stories Make You Memorable

Simmons and many other experts extol story as a way for others to remember people and their messages. Tom Washington, who devotes a full chapter of his 2004 book *Interview Power* to storytelling, asserts that "in less than three minutes, you can tell a powerful story that will make interviewers remember you favorably for days, weeks, or even months after the interview." Similarly, interviewing guru Carole Martin writes, "When someone comes into an interview and begins to tell interesting stories, the interview becomes enjoyable and sometimes even fun. By engaging the interviewer with your stories, you will have a better chance of being remembered and thought of as a serious candidate for the job."

Author Peg Neuhauser writes, "If you want someone to remember information and believe it, your best strategy in almost every case is to give them the information in the form of a story." Indeed, we remember people who tell stories because, as psychologists and neuroscientists tell us, stories form the basis of how we think, organize, and remember information.

Stories Establish Trust

Trust has grown into a significant issue in recruitment. High-profile job seekers who've been caught lying on their resumes are just one reason employers are reluctant to trust job seekers. In 2004, outplacement firm Christian & Timbers researched the resumes of 500 corporate executives and discovered 23 percent of executives lied about their accomplishments. Job seekers can gain an employer's trust by integrating story into a resume, cover letter, or interview. As Simmons writes:

> *Before you attempt to influence anyone, you need to establish enough trust to successfully deliver your message. ... People want to decide these things for themselves ... the best you can do is tell them a story that simulates an experience of your trustworthiness. Hearing your story is as close as they can get to first-hand experience of watching you "walk the walk" as opposed to the "talk the talk." ... You need to tell a story that demonstrates you are the kind of person people can trust.*

Stories establish an emotional connection between the storyteller and the listener and inspire the listener's investment in the storyteller's success. When stories convey moving content and are told with feeling, the listener feels an emotional bond with the storyteller. Often the listener can empathize or relate the story to an aspect of his or her own life. That bond instantly enables the listener to invest emotionally in your success.

The Information Age and the era of knowledge workers might seem cutting edge, but in his popular book *A Whole New Mind*, Daniel Pink asserts that society has moved beyond that mindset and into the Conceptual Age in which we are "creators and empathizers," "pattern recognizers," and "meaning makers." Story is an important tool in this age because it enables us to "encapsulate, contextualize, and emotionalize." Pink refers to story as "context enriched by emotion" and tells us that "story is high touch because stories almost always pack an emotional punch." Gerry Lantz of Stories That Work, a firm that uses stories in branding, compares stories to information, noting that stories are accessible, involving, evocative, meaningful, and a product of the creative right brain, while information is processed through the rational left brain through analysis, interpretation, evaluation, and planning. Both information and stories are necessary.

Stories Help You Stand Out

Consider that many job seekers or coworkers vying for the same position you seek probably have qualifications that are similar to yours. But will they be describing those qualifications to employers in evocative story form? Probably not. If you do, you'll distinguish yourself from those who seek to sell themselves to employers in less engaging ways.

Look around you. Story is everywhere. Increasingly, advertisers are telling stories in TV commercials and print ads. In an age of minuscule attention spans, marketers know that stories are the key to drawing in their audiences and connecting with them emotionally. A growing body of literature describes the link between storytelling and marketing/sales, including an article in which Warren Hersch discusses the value of storytelling in insurance sales ("story-selling" in the words of Mitch Anthony, a financial planner that Hersch quotes). Merely being educated about a product is not enough to motivate a buyer to take significant action, Hersch notes; clients need to be emotionally energized through story. Given that that the intuitive thinking associated with stories leads prospects to conclusions more easily than does analytical thinking, Hersch advises salespeople to "use storytelling to build rapport and credibility with the prospect." Substitute "employer" for "prospect" and "job seekers" for "salespeople," and Hersch's advice about using story in sales becomes instantly applicable to the job seeker selling himself or herself to an employer.

Stories Illustrate What You Have to Offer

Stories illustrate skills, accomplishments, values, characteristics, qualifications, expertise, strengths, and more. Employers don't want to know merely the dry facts of what you've done. They want examples, anecdotes, illustrations—

stories. You can showcase just about any skill with a story. (Chapter 2 tells you more about how to do it.) Washington advises that "using anecdotes to describe job skills is a highly effective interview technique." Truly scrutinizing the stories behind your life and career enables you to recognize patterns that reveal and reinforce who you are, what you can do, how you are qualified, what you know, what you value, what you've learned, what you've accomplished, and what results you'll produce for the employer.

Stories Paint Vivid Pictures

Remember when your parents read or told you stories when you were a child? You undoubtedly visualized the story as a sort of movie in your brain. Job seekers can use colorful and even entertaining stories to imprint lasting visual images onto employers' minds.

Stories Provide Explanations and Reveal Your Response to Change

Stories explain key life/career decisions, choices, and changes. Especially revealing to employers are personal and career stories about coping strategies, risky moves, choices made under pressure, imperfections, and lessons learned from mistakes, failures, and derailments. Chapter 2 explains more about these change stories.

Stories Demonstrate Your Communication Skills

Stories told well help you portray yourself as a strong communicator. Effectively using stories in job seeking venues offers the further benefit of demonstrating your communication skills, which is significant because most employers seek candidates who communicate well. David Boje, a well-known scholar in the organizational-storytelling field, wrote in 1991 that "people who are more skilled as storytellers and story interpreters seem to be more effective communicators than those who are less skilled." Similarly, David Lorenzo, author of *Career Intensity,* notes that "we continue to place a premium on people who have the ability to tell a story."

About This Book

This book is rooted in my dissertation research for my Ph.D. in organizational behavior from Union Institute & University. I've made an exhaustive study of what scholars and experts have to say about the uses of storytelling and how those uses can be applied to the job search and career advancement. I've also interviewed job changers and people in changing organizations as well as conducted focus groups with hiring managers, recruiters, and human resources professionals to obtain their reactions to storytelling in resumes, cover letters, and interviewing.

Here is how the book is organized:

- **Part 1, "Career-Propelling Story Basics":** Explains how to craft stories about accomplishments and skills that employers demand.
- **Part 2, "Using Storytelling in Your Job Search":** Delves into the specifics of integrating stories into networking, resumes, cover letters, interviewing, portfolios, and personal branding.
- **Part 3, "Continuous Career Storytelling":** Describes how you can deploy storytelling within an organization—to advance in that organization as well as to communicate about and cope with change.

Your story is unique and special. My goal is that this book will guide you in telling your story in many ways that will propel your career.

Part 1

Career-Propelling Story Basics

CHAPTER I

The Quintessential "You" Story

Before you begin developing stories that illustrate your skills and accomplishments, you will likely find it useful to develop one or more stories that capture the essence of who you are. Your starting point for all career-propelling stories should be a narrative that truly reveals your character and what makes you unique. The story might disclose what makes you tick, what drives you, what you value, what your goals are, and how you behave in a crisis or a time of change, as Annette Simmons suggests in *The Story Factor.*

You may not use this story in your actual job search, but you'll use it as a starting point to help you get to know yourself better and draw from it to develop additional stories that illustrate skills and accomplishments.

Starting Places for Your "You" Story

This type of "you" story is not my original concept. Simmons coined the "Who Am I Story," while Steve Denning dubs his the "Who Are You Story." Simmons's *The Story Factor* and Denning's *The Leader's Guide to Storytelling* respectively offer excellent techniques for developing these stories.

Denning, for example, suggests as starting points a story about a favorite place of your youth, a story of overcoming adversity or an obstacle, a tale involving someone admirable or influential, or narrative about a significant event from your past. Clearly, "you" stories can come from areas of your life far beyond your work and career; they can come from any part of your experience.

Simmons recommends identifying a quality about yourself and then developing a story about a time you shined with this quality, a time you blew it, a mentor who taught you about the quality, or a book or movie that embodies the quality. Similarly, Joe Lambert, author of the *Digital Storytelling Cookbook*, suggests developing a story about an accomplishment.

Decisive moments, another of Lambert's suggestions, or turning points are also excellent fodder for the Quintessential "You" Story and often originate, as Denning points out, in late adolescent years, when young people are leaving the safety of their families and determining their purpose in life.

Often there's a story behind how you chose your career path (see Shelley's story on page 15). Rob Sullivan, author of *Getting Your Foot in the Door When You Don't Have a Leg to Stand On,* tells the tale of a young woman who told him she wanted to go to nursing school so that she could help others. When Sullivan pressed her, she told the story of spending weeks at her boyfriend's hospital bedside observing the impact nurses had on patients' lives. Sullivan recommends developing stories of choosing your career by identifying how old you were when you first recognized the career interest, specifically what alerted you to your chosen career field, who might have served as a role model for you in choosing this career (for example, one reason I became a writer is that my father was one), and to what extent you've studied this career field in school or taken the initiative to learn about it on your own.

The various types of "prompts" or starting places for the Quintessential "You" Story suggest that you can actually have more than one story. You might want to develop multiple stories that illustrate different aspects of your character.

The experts suggest setting a positive tone for your story. Even if you tell a dark story, explain how you derived something positive from the experience. For example, my son lived a story in which he was traumatized in high school when two friends—star-crossed lovers—committed suicide by throwing themselves in front of a train. Eventually, though, my son gained an appreciation for the joy and exhilaration of being alive and a desire to love and be loved.

Although you may use your Quintessential "You" Story only as a starting point for your own story-development purposes, it's helpful to imagine that the audience for this story is someone who could hire you or who knows someone who could hire you. Think about your best and most relevant skills and accomplishments, as well as your unique selling points that will attract employers.

Sample Quintessential "You" Stories

Whatever prompt or approach you choose to develop your Quintessential "You" Story, the bottom line is that it should convey a strong sense of who you are, the essence of your being, and the core of your character. The following sample stories do just that.

Kellie

I assign my students the task of writing a Quintessential "You" Story. Here is one of my favorites by a student named Kellie:

A few months back I began working at a hospital where my mom has been a nurse for 10 years. I have thought about working in the health care industry for a while, but I was never quite sure it was for me. I received a job as a unit clerk in the Intensive Care Unit/Neuroscience Intensive Care Unit. My job description was to put in doctors' orders for each patient, monitor the patients' EKGs, file papers, answer phones, and keep supplies stocked. Patient care was not a part of my job, but I was always more than willing to help a nurse when needed, knowing that I would learn more about what I wanted to do.

I went to work at 6:30 a.m. as usual and started all of my normal tasks for both units and noticed this little old man waving at me every time I would pass his door. I waved to him a few times with a smile on my face and continued with what I was doing. After about the fourth or fifth wave, I became curious about why he was so interested in waving to me.

I walked into his room and decided I would talk to him to see if maybe he needed something, or if I could get his nurse for him. When I entered the room, he immediately called me Kelsie, which is ironically close to my name, and I had yet to introduce myself. I introduced myself and asked him if he needed any help, and he said no, but I shouldn't play games with him; he knew my name was Kelsie, and he started to laugh. In talking with him for the next few minutes I continued to correct him when he called me by the wrong name, and he continued to correct me.

I left his room with more curiosity as to why he was in the hospital and decided to speak with his nurse and look at his chart. His diagnosis wasn't anything different from most of the older gentlemen we see in the unit. In speaking with his nurse I found out he had Alzheimer's and could remember only a very small piece from his early adulthood.

I went about my work and continued to wave to him when I passed by his room, still a little curious as to why he was calling me Kelsie. After finishing up most of my work for the morning I went and sat in his room and decided to talk with him. He was placed in restraints because of his not knowing where he was and because he was a hazard to himself if he pulled out his lines and possibly harmed those taking care of him.

I sat down, and he once again called me Kelsie, and we began talking about things he could remember from when he was in the Navy and about his family. After being comfortable with him I removed his restraints when he asked and sat him up in bed to make him more comfortable. He was thrilled that he was able to move and talk "like a normal person." I decided to ask him who Kelsie was, and he simply replied, "you know who Kelsie is; it's you, my youngest daughter." I had no idea what to say other than to laugh and continue talking with him.

In the process of our talking, his oldest daughter and son-in-law had walked into the room and were standing behind me listening to our conversation. I introduced myself, and she asked if she could speak with me. I explained to her the situation and she explained his. Her sister Kelsie had died years previous in a car accident, but it was one of the things he couldn't remember. She told me I had a strong resemblance to her sister and asked if I would mind talking with him as though I were Kelsie to make him happy for the short time he would still be alive.

I happily agreed and continued talking with him every chance I got, listening to all the stories of him and his daughter Kelsie (me). I showed up one day to meet with him and instead I found an empty room and heart to go along with it. One of the nurses approached me and handed me a note addressed to me. His oldest daughter wanted to let me know he had passed away yesterday and his last words were that he loved each and every one of them and to tell Kelsie he loved her as well. Tears of joy and sorrow streamed down my face. I was sad he had gone, but more than that I was happy he had the chance to talk to "Kelsie" before he went.

What do we learn about Kellie from this story?

- She is compassionate.
- She is curious and eager to learn.
- She cares enough about patients to go far beyond the requirements of her job to give them comfort.

If Kellie stated on her resume or in an interview that she is curious, eager to learn, compassionate, and dedicated to patient care, none of those claims would be as believable or compelling as telling this story. She might not ever be in a situation to tell this entire story during her job search, but by developing the story as a first step, she has gotten to know herself better and identified some of the key characteristics about herself that she will want to feature in her job search.

Let's look at more sample Quintessential "You" stories. Like Kellie's story, these are poignant. But notice that unlike Kellie's story, these spell out the "moral" or lesson learned. If you compare them with Kellie's story, you might discover that sometimes the story is actually more powerful if the audience is left to draw its own conclusions about the characteristics exemplified. The audience does not necessarily need to be hit over the head with what the story means.

Abbie

Abbie's story reveals how she learned to embrace being outside her comfort zone after her first public-speaking experience:

> *My hands were shaky and palms were sweaty as I walked up to the podium at the Rotary Club's biweekly meeting. I was presented an award as my middle school's eighth-grade Student of the Month and asked to give a brief speech to the members. It was my first speech in front of a crowd of people, and after being home-schooled in seventh grade, I had become very introverted and uneasy around large groups of people. My heart raced as I began the first sentence of my speech. "I would like to thank the Ro-Ro-Rotary Club...." Oh no! I had already made a mistake, and I had not even finished the first sentence. My mind raced, and all I could think about was how embarrassing it was to mess up the very name of the club that was giving me an award.*
>
> *Afterwards, I stayed around to talk to a few of the Rotarians. Their reactions to my speech were completely opposite from what I had expected. Instead of mentioning my mispronunciation of the Rotary Club's name, they congratulated me and said how well I did. I was confused by their kindness, but began to feel a little bit better about my actions. It was that day that I realized I had a lot of work to do. I knew that if I wanted to pursue a career in business, I needed to become much more comfortable giving presentations and talking among crowds of people.*
>
> *After the Rotary Club speech, I began purposely putting myself in uncomfortable situations that required an extroverted personality. Soon, I was elected to the Florida Business Leaders of America district vice president, which required me to talk in front of groups of 200 students or more. I was also elected president of the student body, where it was necessary to remain in constant contact with the students, principal, and administration of the school.*
>
> *During my senior year of high school, I was again selected as the Rotary Club Student of the Month and asked to speak at one of the Rotary Club's meetings. This time, instead of being nervous, I was confident and excited to give my speech to the members. I knew this speech would be a great test to prove to myself how far I had come since eighth grade. I walked up to the lectern, said the first few sentences, and was completely comfortable with the situation. During the speech, I even told a joke and improvised part of it on the spot. It was at that moment that I realized that people could change; it is just a matter of how badly one wants to.*
>
> *The hardest thing a person can do is change an aspect of himself or herself and make it last. Anyone can wake up and decide, "Today I am going to be nice for a change." However, it is the days afterwards that make the difference. Changing oneself can be even more complex when one does not feel the need to do so. I found myself in this situation after giving my first speech at the Rotary Club. I was comfortable with being shy and introverted; however, I knew this personality*

trait would not bring success in the future. This speech marked a milestone in my life because I realized how beneficial it often is to step outside my comfort zone.

Craig

Craig's story discloses his deeply rooted commitment to teamwork, motivational skills, and doing what it takes to succeed.

During my earlier days I was an avid soccer player; I lived for early Saturday mornings. Getting up early to get my equipment together, lacing up my cleats, and experiencing the fellowship that I got from my teammates were unsurpassable. However, it was not all fun and games on the field. As team captain I had a duty and responsibility to my team to make sure we were achieving our goals through a strong work ethic and a strong commitment to our team.

Throughout the season I was there to will on my team through my words and my actions and our 1996 county championship game was no different. It was a rainy day, and the turf was heavy. Our opponents were strong and had beaten us earlier in the season. The first half of the game was a battle. Players were working hard for each other, and no one was willing to give an inch. Just before halftime our opponents scored, and my teammates were downhearted. The halftime whistle blew, and we headed to the locker room. Inside I looked around and said, "What's wrong with you guys? We still have another half to go, and we can beat these guys. Come on; this is our time to shine. We worked too hard to just give up now." After a couple of seconds one of my teammates looked up and said, "The big fella is right. We can win this. We played them off the park, and they got a lucky goal." I chimed in again and said, "If you believe, you can do it, and we will do it. Give yourselves the chance to be heroes on this day."

We went out for the second half and got a goal. However, as I went to clear a ball from a penalty box, an opponent stomped on my foot. I knew something was wrong and crawled off the field. Our trainer looked at my foot and said that I had broken my toe. We had used all of our substitutes, so if I came off the field I would leave my team a man down. I looked at the trainer and asked him to tape it up so that I could get out on the field to play. As I walked on the field the trainer told me that I could hurt myself even more, and I looked around and said, "I am needed on the field. If I go off, the team will lose confidence, and they could fold. I can't let that happen. I won't let it happen." I continued to play in pain, and the game finished in a draw leading to extra time.

Playing through the pain, I kept going and tried to keep a brave face on for my team. All the players knew I was hurting, and they knew that I was not willing to give up on them. As we pushed on, the game finished 1–1, and we went to penalties. I was dreading having to take one, so I said that I should go before the goalkeepers take theirs. Penalty after penalty went in until our opponents took their 10th penalty. Their player stepped up and hit the bar, making it 9–8 on penalties. So, I walked up and placed the ball on the penalty spot. Then I heard the whistle and ran up to strike the ball. After planting my bad foot, I could not bear to stand up because I was in so much pain. I fell down and did not see if the ball went in. When I first heard the players and crowd, I thought that I had let the team down and I just started saying, "I'm sorry lads, I blew it." Then I heard, "what are you talking about? We won the game." When I looked up I saw the ball in the net and all my teammates around me saying that they were glad I kept going and that without me they would never have done it.

I always pride myself on being there for my friends and being dependable no matter what I need to do. That day will always be special to me for I know that I never let them down and that I was willing to do anything to help our team achieve its goal.

Shelley

Shelley's story illustrates how an early event that affected a family member set Shelley on her career path.

Everyone has a childhood memory that influences the choices that they make and alters the path that they take in life. This is my story that influenced my life decisions.

I can still remember August of 1995; it was my favorite time of the year because all the neighborhood children would gather at the pool and go swimming. I was swimming underwater watching all the kids play, but my sister is the person who stood out`to me. I can still picture the sparkle of her tears rolling down her face while she sat on the pool steps watching all the other kids have fun. The situation that led to my sister's anguish happened three months earlier.

In May, my mom decided to take my sister and me to a new lake the city just built. My sister went swimming that day. Afterwards she started feeling sick. The next day at school my sister was playing the telephone game at school, and one of the kids whispered a word in her ear, but my sister couldn't hear her, so she whispered again, and she still couldn't hear her. My sister realized that there was something wrong with her ears. After school my mom took my sister to the doctor, who discovered that she had bacteria in her ears that was causing tumors. Water-borne bacteria that cause such conditions are a risk in contaminated water. I was furious that the city had not taken precautions to ensure the lake water was safe. Over the next couple of months my sister had to get numerous operations on her ears, but the damage was too severe. After numerous operations my sister lost complete hearing in her left ear and partial hearing in her right ear.

To this day my sister still cannot get her ears wet because the tumors could grow back. She has had to live with difficulties that the hearing loss caused in school and in her personal life. Because of the lack of government regulation and laws, my sister lost her hearing. That memory has shaped my decision to try to become a lawyer, so I can fight for people's rights and bring justice to people who cause harm to individuals. That experience has caused me to work harder in school so I can become an attorney. It gave me the determination, drive, strength, and passion to excel so I do not disappoint future clients, my sister, or myself.

Matt

Matt's story demonstrates his persistence.

One month, during my apprenticeship under a Korean master potter, I experienced a great deal of bad luck with the pieces I was making, mostly smaller pieces. Thunder shook the studio enough to knock one piece off a shelf during a storm; another piece melted onto mine in the kiln. For the next month I worked on the biggest and best piece I had ever made. It took an entire month for this one piece alone. One day, I came in to put the finishing touches on it before it would be ready to be fired. My streak of bad luck had not ended because I came in to find a pile of clay pieces from my collapsed artwork. I found out that the clay I had used was bad and, of course, decided to find a new, more reliable clay company to buy my clay from.

So after a month of work all gone down the drain on what was to be the best piece I had ever made at the time, my persistence and commitment to excellence would not let me give up, even in what seemed like the worst streak of luck in the world. I was disappointed and frustrated, and at the point where most people might have just given up entirely, but I used it to fuel my goal of making the piece even better this time. I took another month working from scratch with new clay from the beginning all over again. I finally finished it.

This time, the piece was even bigger, and even better than what it would have been before. I put everything I had into it and was extremely pleased with the final product. I ended up being able to put this piece in many art shows and won several awards and scholarships for it. I had many people eager to buy it, for over $1,000 even, but I wasn't ready to let go of a piece that I could still profit from in shows and scholarships. I earned the highest award from a local organization and earned a scholarship, as well as a space in the window of a prestigious downtown art gallery.

This experience reaffirms for me that I should never give up on any goal I have for myself and that I'm capable of getting through anything I put myself up against. My persistence and goal-focused drive keep me thriving in a world of uncontrollable factors and setbacks. My ability to work through any circumstance and solve problems got me to a finished product that I could be proud of and that could even help pay for my college experience.

Andy

Andy's dramatic post-hurricane story describes the gratification gained from helping in a time of crisis.

> *In the fall of 2004, the beginning of my senior year of high school, hurricanes Charley, Frances, Ivan, and Jeanne pounded the state of Florida. My hometown is centrally located between the east and west coasts, sheltered by miles of land from tidal surges and the fiercest winds of the storms. However, that is not to say that we went unaffected. The days before and after the brunt of the storms were still plagued with incessant rain. One or possibly two storms in a season would have caused no serious problem; that would have been normal. But four? The infrastructure of the city was not designed to withstand so much rain and wind in such a short time. By the time the third storm approached, parking lots and streets were under water. Neighborhoods around town were flooded, cars were submerged, and trees were uprooting from the completely saturated soil.*
>
> *My father and I decided to drive through the neighborhood just down the road from our house and see what damage the storm had done to our area. As we drove along the streets there was not too much to see. There were some downed trees in yards, leaves and small branches everywhere, and flooded ditches. As we neared the back of the neighborhood I noticed a group of two or three men working with buckets, brooms, and a small pump on generator power to move the runoff water that was approaching a house. In an instant my father and I recognized one of the men and stopped immediately. The man so desperately trying to save his house from flooding was my dentist, Dr. Dutter. He has been my dentist as long as I can remember. I rode the same bus as two of his daughters in elementary school. We got out, and Dr. Dutter came to greet us in the midst of his frantic effort to save his house (uninsured from floods) from the rising water. The problem was that they were unable to move the water fast enough and far enough away to make any progress.*
>
> *I immediately headed back to my house where I grabbed a bucket and some old pool vacuum hose that we could attach to the pump and move the water across the street and into a ditch that drained into the woods. Even with all our efforts, the water still crept toward the low-lying house. One of Dr. Dutter's friends called the industrial equipment rental places around town in search of a stronger pump. To give an idea of what we were working with at the time, it would have been just as effective to siphon the water with a garden hose. Only one place on the other side of town had a pump, a brand new one at that, but it came with a catch. They had received a new pump without a new hose to fit it. Not only that, but Dr. Dutter had no car as his family members had grabbed their valuables and fled to his in-laws' house. If that weren't enough, the rental store closed in less than an hour, and the house was sure to flood with nobody there to bail away the water.*

I volunteered to drive Dr. Dutter across town in my truck in what seemed like a desperate attempt to save his house from flooding. We were fortunate enough to make it before the store closed. We went to pick up the pump in hopes that we would come across some hosing that fit it, or maybe someone would turn some back in by the time we got there. Unfortunately, there was no hosing at the rental center. The trip appeared to be in vain. Fortunately, a contractor who happened to be a regular customer came in and the store manager told him our situation. I still think it was a divine act of God that the customer had a spare hose that fit the pump. He headed back to his shop and within half an hour we had a pump and free hose. A total stranger's willingness to help made me proud of my community and how the people there come together in times of hardship and celebration alike.

We hurried back to Dr. Dutter's house, our spirits lifted, to set up the industrial sump pump. I spent the rest of the day wading into dirty water, setting up the pump, and bailing water with a five-gallon bucket to save the house of a man I see once every six months. As darkness fell, my dad (unable to help much himself because of a bad back) returned to see how things were going. Dr. Dutter began praising me and thanking us for our help, telling my dad how much help I had been and how impressed he was with me. It was embarrassing to hear him say all that in front of me. I could only think that I had done what anyone would have in the same situation, and I still think that. I was just happy to help him and be a good neighbor. His house was safe from flooding, at least until the next hurricane season, and I felt a great sense of pride and accomplishment to have been a part of that.

Not too much later a thank-you note came to me in the mail with a gift certificate to a sporting-goods store. The note was nice, and I was glad to hear he decided to buy flood insurance for next year, but I was almost ashamed to take the gift card. My decision to help him was not based on the assumption of compensation. I did it only because I knew he needed my help, and it was the right thing to do. Of course, I dared not insult him by refusing the gift. I managed to put it to good use. When I think about that day, I always remember how grateful he was for my help, and how surprised he seemed to be that a teenager would spend his day off from school to help him bail water and chase down a sump pump and a hose. That memory of helping someone who needed and appreciated it so much is a reward that will last my entire life and remind me forever how fulfilling it is to come together and accomplish something meaningful.

Summary

In developing your foundational story, ask yourself, what story can I tell that best captures the quintessential me? (And, as mentioned earlier, you may find that you need more than one story to express the quintessential you.) Develop that story or stories, and the stories in chapter 2 and beyond will be much easier to generate.

How to Develop Career-Propelling Stories

After building the Quintessential "You" stories you saw in chapter 1, you need to know how to develop stories about skills, abilities, expertise, personal traits and characteristics, values, and accomplishments. But how do you develop the stories, how do you know which of these qualities to develop stories about, and how do you know how to frame your stories?

This chapter suggests formulas for career-propelling stories and shows how you might use them in specific job search communications (resumes, cover letters, and interview responses). It guides you in determining which skills to showcase in your stories and provides suggestions for framing your stories. The end of the chapter focuses on developing stories to illustrate specific skills, especially the all-important ability to handle change. First, you need to know how to formulate or structure a story.

Formulas for Structuring Your Story

Career experts have developed myriad formulas and clever acronyms for how to structure stories to be used in the job search. These formulas have in common the idea of setting the scene for your story by describing the situation, problem, or challenge you faced; explaining what action you took to address the situation, solve the problem, or meet the challenge; and explaining the result of your actions. Results expressed quantitatively, in numbers and percents, for example, are especially effective. Optionally you could add what you learned or gained from this experience.

Some of the common story formulas that experts use, expressed as acronyms, include the following (note that some of the formulas are in common usage, and their originators are unknown, whereas others are associated with specific originators as shown):

- **CAR:** Challenge, Action, Result
- **CCAR:** Context, Challenge, Action, Result (developed by Kathryn Troutman)

- **PAR:** Problem, Action, Result
- **PARLA:** Problem, Action, Result, Learning, Application (developed by Donald Asher)
- **SAR:** Situation, Action, Result
- **SCARQ:** Situation, Challenge, Action, Results-Quantified (developed by Steve Gallison)
- **SHARE:** Situation, Hindrance, Action, Results, Evaluation (developed by Fred Coon)
- **SIA:** Situation, Impact, Analysis
- **SMART:** Situation with Metrics (or Situation and More), Actions, Results, Tie-in (developed by Susan Britton Whitcomb)
- **SOAR:** Situation, Obstacle, Action, Result
- **STAR:** Situation, Task, Action, Result

Carole Martin, in her book *Boost Your Interview IQ*, also lists CAB (Challenge, Action, Behavior), SBO (Situation, Behavior, Outcome), SAO (Situation, Action, Outcome), and SPARE (Situation or Problem, Action, Result, Enthusiasm). These story formulas are most often prescribed for interviews; thus, you can find a story example for each in chapter 7 on interview stories.

Develop stories of various lengths and containing assorted amounts of detail for each element of your job search.

Structuring Resume Stories

Develop a short bullet-point version of your story for your resume. Because a resume needs to attract attention quickly, it's a good idea to tell each story so that the result comes first, as in the following bullets about a job seeker's multipart accomplishment:

- Beat two-month deadline for operationalizing online scheduling, time/attendance, and payroll system by overseeing fast-track implementation from outside vendor.
- Reduced payroll discrepancies 25 percent and time spent scheduling employees and resolving timesheet-related issues by 50 percent.
- Decreased time spent on reports by 25 percent by customizing reports to track labor/benefits allocation.
- Earned vendor's Certificate for Management's Commitment for Successful Implementation and Design Contribution to Improve Efficiencies.

Read more about resume storytelling in chapter 4.

Structuring Cover Letter Stories

Develop a more detailed paragraph version of your story for your cover letters. In the following example, the same story is told in paragraph form in the job seeker's cover letter. Note that a cover letter should not rehash the resume, so even if you are highlighting the same accomplishment in both documents, vary your language and the way you frame the story.

> *I demonstrated my strong project-management skills when the project team I led exceeded all expectations while implementing an outside vendor's system for online scheduling, time/attendance, and payroll. Not only did we crush our two-month deadline, but we also reduced payroll discrepancies, slashed in half the time spent scheduling employees and resolving timesheet-related issues, and cut time spent on reports. The icing on the cake was earning the vendor's Certificate for Management's Commitment for Successful Implementation and Design Contribution to Improve Efficiencies.*

Read more about cover letter stories in chapter 5.

Structuring Job Interview Stories

You'll need to develop a still more detailed version, composed in a conversational style, for job interviews.

> *My company was struggling with scheduling employees, monitoring their time and attendance, as well as tying these elements into payroll. We needed a system, preferably online, that would make these tasks more efficient, save time, and reduce errors. When management decided to go with an outside vendor for the new system, they chose me to head up the project team. We were on a tight, two-month deadline, but I led the team to surpass not only the deadline, but the expected results. Under my guidance, we got the vendor's system online so successfully that we reduced payroll discrepancies by 25 percent. Since we've operationalized it, the company has saved time in scheduling employees and resolving timesheet-related issues; in fact, these processes take half the time they used to. By customizing reports to track labor and benefits allocation, we also cut time spent on reports by a quarter. We did such a great job and made the functions so much more efficient that the vendor recognized us with its Certificate for Management's Commitment for Successful Implementation and Design Contribution to Improve Efficiencies.*

Read more about interviewing stories in chapter 7.

Identifying Characteristics to Highlight in Your Stories

Once you're familiar with the basic accomplishments-driven job-search story structures, the next step is to determine what characteristics you want to showcase about yourself in your stories. The answer is to tell stories that demonstrate the skills, abilities, values, and knowledge that employers seek in the type of job and industry you're targeting. Here's how to do so:

1. Identify a dozen or so help-wanted ads or Internet job postings that typify the kind of job you seek.
2. List keywords that describe the skills and characteristics required for these jobs. (See page 36 for a list of skills and characteristics that employers typically seek.)
3. Now, highlight all the skills and characteristics keywords the ads or job postings have in common and make a list of these frequently appearing skills/characteristics.
4. For each skill/characteristic listed, compose a story that illustrates how you have successfully demonstrated that skill or characteristic in your career, or even in your personal life.
5. Be sure to compose stories that come from a variety of aspects of your life and career; don't focus on just one job or extracurricular activity, for example. Draw your stories from fairly recent experience. Employers want to know what you've done lately that could benefit their organization.

Story-Framing Devices

Keeping in mind that a successful story must be true and told in context, consider these ideas for framing your stories so that they come from various perspectives:

- A time in your life when this skill/characteristic was tested.
- A person/event in your life that taught you the importance of this skill/characteristic.
- A time when you failed to live up to this skill/characteristic and decided never to let it happen again.
- A movie/story/book/event that exemplifies this skill/characteristic for you.

  (The above four come from Annette Simmons in her books, *The Story Factor* and *Whoever Tells the Best Story Wins.)*
- A turning point in your development of this skill/characteristic.
- A story of using this skill/characteristic in overcoming one or more obstacles (suggested by Stephen Denning in *The Leader's Guide to Storytelling).*

- A Cinderella story of having been an underdog who used this skill/characteristic to emerge triumphant.
- A hero story in which you used this skill/characteristic to do something unexpected to save the day.
- A humorous and probably self-deprecating way you've used this skill/characteristic.

  (The above three are from David Lorenzo in *Career Intensity.)*
- A story about tasks and job functions related to this skill/characteristic.
- A timeline of how you developed and sharpened this skill/characteristic.
- An example from your personal life (as opposed to career) of deploying this skill/characteristic.
- Patterns that have emerged in your development of this skill/characteristic.
- Results you've achieved through using this skill/characteristic.
- Lessons you've learned while developing and using this skill/characteristic.
- Ways you've applied this skill/characteristic in diverse situations.
- A strength or vulnerability from your past that led to developing this skill/characteristic.
- A time when you felt passionate and alive in your work (and the skill/characteristic that made the feeling possible).
- One or more stories that you find yourself repeatedly telling about your work (identify the recurring skill[s] or characteristic[s] in these stories).
- If you could tell just one story to explain what you do in your work, what would it be, and what skill or characteristic would it involve)?

  (The above three come from Cathryn Wellner in the section "Story Prompts," from *Wake Me Up When the Data Is Over: How Organizations Use Stories to Achieve Results,* edited by Lori Silverman.)

Following are examples of stories that use some of these frameworks. The first one recognizes a characteristic that has become a career pattern:

I have learned that my role is to do work that makes a difference in people's lives. For the first 20 years, I worked in television news, believing in the peoples' right to know. For the past six years, I've been in education, helping teachers and their students. My ultimate goal is to be head of a department.

This one describes a skill honed in personal life rather than career:

I realized I had solid problem-solving skills during my freshman year after I went to the soup kitchen in Parkersburg to serve food to the less fortunate. I felt that I needed to do something more, so I had an idea that when everybody moved out of the dorms at the end of a semester, instead of throwing nonperishable food away, students could put it in a box, and I would take it to the local food bank so it could feed the poor. I ended up gathering about six carloads of canned and dry food that would have been thrown away.

The next story describes failure to live up to a skill/characteristic and the determination never to let it happen again:

My leadership skills were called into question by my first evaluation as a district manager. I was rated much lower than I had ever been rated. I realized that, after having been promoted into a new position, I needed to learn a lot more. Determined to never again get a low rating, I learned as much as I possibly could, and this quest for knowledge became the driving force behind my attaining the high rating I achieved for this year.

Here's a story that describes a time when a skill was tested:

I solve problems every day in my job, but one recent example I had that truly tested my problem-solving skills involved a woman who called me to question why we refunded part of her premium to her. She's a new policy-holder who was quoted $2,900 for an annual premium and paid that amount, but in the computer, her annual premium was about $2,500, so we refunded her the difference. My first hunch was she received a discount for paying in full, but when I calculated the discount percent, it was not adding up. After about two or three iterations of trying various combinations of discounts, I still was unable to figure out why the quote and actual premium were different and figured I was not looking for the right root cause. I decided to manually price her policy from the ground up. During the process I happened to notice that her birthday on her application was written ambiguously and could have been interpreted as 1925 or 1928. I calculated quotes for both ages and realized the reason for the difference. I honored the lower rate since the payment transactions were fully completed.

The next story describes a turning point/event that taught the importance of a skill/characteristic:

As an undergrad, I took a course on argument and advocacy and learned a very important concept called Tooling Modeling, which is a logical way of thinking with three parts: claim, grounds, and warrant. The claim is your point; the grounds consist of your proof, evidence, or backing; and your warrant is your logical leap that connects the two. The theory is naturally a little more complicated than that, but this way of thinking has been my bible for rational thought and was the single most valuable lesson I learned in college. I use this way of thinking when I am presented with problems that require decisions. I structure a rational, logical argument for each likely outcome. I can therefore see where weaknesses exist, either in the grounds or the warrant. I conduct a bump-and-compare between arguments to see which are the strongest, and I go with the most durable argument. I also take a practical approach to decision making in that I try to find out the best outcome for the least price or cost.

Finally, here's a story framed up to identify a strength from the past that led to developing this skill/characteristic:

I have always had a fascination for how machines work, and whenever my family and I went on vacation, I would always try and get the window seat on the plane, if only to watch the flaps and air-brakes in action during takeoff and landing. As I continued my education, I felt a compulsion to use my degree in a people-oriented profession. So, while I love machines, I'd like to contribute my engineering skills in a company that affects people's lives positively. I just like helping people.

Telling Stories About Handling Change

It's important to be able to tell stories about a wide variety of skills, characteristics, and values, but "change skills" are arguably the most important because they also encompass many other skills that employers seek. The job seeker or worker who can successfully convey—through stories—his or her ability to lead, communicate, and handle organizational change has an advantage over other job seekers and workers.

Here's why: Where stability was once the goal of organizations, relentless change is now the constant. Scholars characterize change today as no longer an option but a necessity. Without change, organizations lack the competitive and visionary edge they need to succeed. Some experts compare the current age of profound organizational change to the Industrial Revolution. The pace of change, greater than at any time in history, has compounded the challenge for organizations, with leaders noting a striking increase in the frequency and velocity of change. Where new ideas in the form of products or services took six years to enter the marketplace in 1966 and 18 months in 1996, they now take five months, noted, J. W. Moran and J. M. Mead in *The TQM Magazine* in 2001.

The Causes of Change

What's responsible for this inexorable change? Here are a few real stories that illustrate some of the major causes.

Business Process Redesign/Reengineering

I was team leader for a reengineering project. My team was responsible for change management for the implementation. We had no in-house change-management expertise, so a consulting firm had promised to bring in an expert to assist with design and development for change and then transfer the knowledge to provide us with the in-house expertise we needed for the ongoing rollout. As the design and development of the implementation phase progressed, the huge amount of change that would need management became alarmingly clear. The consulting firm failed to provide the change-management expert. Since I was responsible for this aspect of the project, and change management was not being properly addressed, I began to be scapegoated, and I truly began to fear for my job. The project was in jeopardy of failing because of the consulting firm's failure to provide the appropriate level of expertise. Ultimately, the desired results were not achieved. I've therefore learned to trust my instincts and gain support of others earlier so I won't be scapegoated for the lack of expertise needed to make the change. I am also willing to obtain additional training so I can be the one with the expertise.

Change in Organization Ownership

I worked on the sale of the company for six months before the other employees knew about it. I'm very good at getting the job done, no matter what, with or without help. Then I adapt to change if something falls through.

Employee Turnover, Especially in Management

In the department I was with, product management, the average number of bosses within a one-year period could be anywhere from 4 to 10. In the two years I've been there, I've gone through five bosses. So if anything can exemplify dealing with change and coping with change and rolling with the punches, I think that's as clearly as it comes. My previous boss had 12 bosses within the year. There's a very quick and constant turnaround. People hone in on the skills needed for the department. You're assigned to a project, and you have to learn everything there is to know about that specific area—and then another department will want that skill set. They'll say, "Can we steal that person?" And that person ends up leaving. Or that person transfers into another department.

Changing Technology

Management completely changed the whole back source of our project. We had to redo all of our code and everything. So in handling that situation, we had a change-management plan to do things on a certain timeline and meet our goals. We divided the task up among various people and assigned responsibilities.

Loss of Customer Base

> *Our college has lost considerable enrollment, so I have been striving to be a change agent for every student by personally giving one-on-one customer service to aid retention. I try to explain to each student what he or she needs to know to get admitted and obtain financial aid, and they always end up coming back to see me. I'm learning how to adapt to doing more work as a one-person office while the VP keeps demanding "fix it, fix enrollment, fix it, change anything that needs changing." I have to find every possible way to be more productive without getting any more staff.*

Observers and researchers also cite global competition, flattening hierarchies, quality-improvement programs, burgeoning entrepreneurial initiatives, increasing diversity, cost reduction, lean production, heightened customer expectations and the subsequent drive for improved customer service, deregulation, privatization, expanded financial resources, a blurring of industry distinctions, and an eroding of the divide between industrial and service businesses as drivers of change. In addition, outsourcing and offshoring, with their accompanying downsizing, have become accepted management tools. Even the nonprofit sector is not immune to change; it is subject to funding cuts, new clients, and the need to dramatically increase services.

Although much change is directed at improving organizational profitability, some stems from the disruptive turmoil of unexpected events such as the September 11, 2001, terrorist attacks; Hurricane Katrina; the SARS outbreak; the Northeast power-grid failure of 2003; and the financial collapse of 2008. Looming external drivers of change might include soaring fuel prices and the threat of a pandemic. In this sample story, September 11 led to company downsizing:

> *Early in my tenure in the training and development department of a large hospitality company, 9-11 temporarily killed the tourism industry, and we had to go through some downsizing. My role was to work with other members of the leadership team to make some tough decisions and to think through some criteria about how we would make those decisions—to make sure that we were being fair and open with everyone. People in training and development are almost always the first to go. We tried to think about the human factor and to be creative in considering the individuals, evaluating the situations, and coming up with criteria.*

Storytelling provides an innovative way for careerists to enter organizations and to thrive within ever-changing organizations. Change supplies an advantageous backdrop for storytelling. To garner more ideas for the kinds of skills and aptitudes around which you can tell change stories, see Carol Goman's Change-Adept Questionnaire at http://www.ckg.com/change_questionnaire.html.

Stories That Exemplify Change Skills

You can distinguish yourself from the competition by, for example, telling stories in resumes and cover letters, as well as during job interviews, of how you have embraced change as an opportunity instead of an obstacle, as in these next examples.

I was a consultant for a company that had been under the umbrella of a large government contractor which decided to sell off its commercial division to focus on its military applications. A venture-capital group came along and bought the company, which then lost its controller to the original owner, the government contractor. The newly purchased company had tried to replace the controller, but the new hires just didn't stick. It was a very challenging environment. I was there for six months and got them through their first year-end close and their first audit as the new company. I stayed with them long enough to where they got their new controller on board, and I got him settled in for a couple of months and fully trained. As a consultant you have to be smart and fast because the client wants to see results quickly. You've got to be able to very quickly absorb the basic organizational structure and learn the key players. Then you have to quickly learn their software and processes—and look for ways to improve them.

The strategic repositioning and closing of the training center where I am director of organizational development has been a significant change. A major contributor to the stress has been the high level of ambiguity during the past year and the fact that people are at different places in the grief and transition process at the same time. My style in times of stress and ambiguity is to try and find something productive I can do both personally and for the larger community. So, I have chosen to deal with this change by being proactive and leading an effort to offer career-enrichment programs at our sister training center. I've also collaborated with outside vendors to design a development program to support supervisors and staff through this transition, provided one-on-one coaching for the center's leadership, and provided individual sessions for teams. These sessions have been well attended, and I've received very positive and appreciative comments from staff members who attended them.

In my current job, I am working on a project to increase efficiencies in the customer-service area, one component of which is to better control the way customer service handles the mail. I questioned the administrative clerk, who's responsible for receiving and distributing the mail, about how she does her job. She gathers mail from the P.O. box, reads the recipient, and passes mail around to be handled. I asked her what would happen if mail is lost. How would we track it? If someone doesn't handle the sender's inquiry in a timely manner, how can we know? I presented with her many questions of real and hypothetical situations where the ball was dropped somewhere so I could find out from her if she had a plan in place to deal with those situations. The clerk at first felt confident in her work, took great pride in being industrious, and didn't feel passing mail around was a broken process, but after our conversation, she began to see the situation from my point of view and became receptive to new ideas and change. I needed and attained her buy-in so that I could create change and add value to her job. Together, we've developed a process to ensure that customer inquiries don't slip through the cracks.

The bank in which I worked instituted a policy that centralized the lending process. An application was to be taken from the client and sent off to be approved or declined, processed, prepared, and returned to the branch to be signed by the client. While the process was streamlined, it also took away valuable face-to-face knowledge about the client and the loan. If the employee did not have any prior lending experience, he or she couldn't answer simple loan questions from the client. While I appreciated the newly created time in my schedule, I felt that the clients were being slighted. I proposed to my boss a small adjustment that would permit brief face time with the client. My boss implemented my idea, and now we have the best of both worlds, face-to-face time with clients without taking significant time away from the streamlined process.

In my senior campaign-management job, I was the pinnacle person for a diverse group of project managers. I had many representatives from all the product bases constantly coming to me to develop databases of customers they could sell to. They wanted to know who they could market to. I would collaborate with them, asking questions like, "what's the budget, how many pieces do you want to direct mail? Or do you want to call these people? What media will you use?" I worked to ensure each group got all the demographics it wanted. I'd pull the requirements into the data. And I'll be darned if the group didn't change its mind and ask for a different demographic. Or something unpredictable like a hurricane would mean the group couldn't mail to a certain region. So, I'd have to throw all the data back into the pond and re-fish. And the changes wouldn't happen with just one group; they would happen with all of them at one time. I dreaded my pager going off at 7 a.m. because a project manager had a thought while sleeping last night: "Ooh, I would love to see how many prospective customers wear toenail polish." But whatever their requirement was, I said, "I'm on top of it." I enjoyed the analytic aspects and the busyness and the constant go, go, go. Change drives me. It's something I enjoy because it's an extra challenge.

Some change isn't instigated by the organization at all, but by the employee who decides to change careers, an increasingly common phenomenon. In listing 21st-century human-resources trends, nonprofit CEO John McMorrow predicted that career change would become the rule rather than the exception, in part because of the "erosion of the implied good-faith contract between employer and employee." Career-changers, too, should be prepared to tell deft stories of why they made the change and how they've adapted, as in this example:

> *I made the huge change from litigation to transactional work and from private practice to being an in-house attorney. I was previously doing high-stakes litigation, most of it out of state. I did all the behind-the-scenes work—all the drafting, all the research—which I didn't find exciting. I would have liked to be in court arguing, but I was spending 11 hours a day or so in front of my computer researching and writing. I didn't like writing those long memoranda and motions. Transactional work is different. I like it better because I deal with discrete issues. I meet with clients almost every day to see what their needs are for a particular transaction. They are internal clients, such as people in the marketing department. I haven't gotten bored. I'm very happy. This may be one of the first times I've felt excited about going to work.*

You can find some additional career-change stories at the Web site of DBM, a global human-capital management-services firm. Although the purpose of the stories is to promote DBM's services, the storytelling in them provides some good models:
www.dbm.com/content.aspx?main=30&item=31#CareerTransitions.
More change-story examples appear in chapters 3 through 7.

Telling compelling stories as you transition from one role to the next, and one organization to the next, helps the listener feel invested in your success, a scenario that bodes well when the storyteller is a job seeker and the listener is an employer, contend *Harvard Business Review* writers Ibarra and Lineback. The authors describe a worker who developed and told change stories about a bankruptcy, a turnaround, and a rapid reorganization, eventually garnering referrals to employers and job interviews. In another example, a worker learned more about her career passions and became more committed to a planned career change each time she told her story by writing a cover letter, participating in a job interview, or networking with friends.

Examples of Change Skills

Change skills should be a major focus of the stories you tell as you progress from one organization to the next. Here's how scholars and experts characterize these skills:

- A passion for the vision
- Ability to determine a transformational strategy
- Ability to develop trust
- Ability to foster and create an atmosphere that enables people to test new situations, generate recommendations, experiment with new ways of operating, and exhibit some dysfunctional behavior while new equilibrium takes root in the culture

- Ability to frame change in terms of organizational results, as well as the effect on the individual
- Ability to install leadership processes
- Ability to interact with individuals and groups in the organization to explain the who, what, when, where, why, and how of the change
- Ability to lead change effort with every word and deed and serve as an organizational role model
- Ability to speak the languages ("organizational dialects") of socio-technical systems, marketing, manufacturing, finance, human resources, and legal
- Ability to stake rewards on results
- Ability to
    - Create
    - Innovate
    - Experiment
    - Take risks
- Ability to work across functions
- Ability to work without management sanction
- Action orientation
- Alertness to early signs of discontinuity, disruption, threat, or opportunity
- Ambition and personal risk
- Analytical skills, especially in analyzing workflow, systems, and finance
- Being a
    - Flexible driver
    - Determined contributor
    - Pain absorber
    - Political manipulator
    - Career enhancer
- Business knowledge
- Capacity to learn from personal experience and the experience of others
- Clear focus on desired achievement balanced against an understanding of where the organization is going

- Collaboration
- Competence concerning
    - Goals
    - Roles
    - Communication
    - "Managing up"
- Confidence
- Constant dedication to making change a reality
- Continuous improvement
- Coping
- Creativity
- Customer service and the ability to develop new perspectives for satisfying customers
- Determination
- Drive to go beyond one's job as directed by organizational needs
- Enthusiasm for change
- Excellent communication skills
- Exceptional combinations of
    - Leadership
    - Managerial skills
    - Technical skills
- Flexibility
- Good corporate citizenship unconstrained by current practices and procedures
- High tolerance for ambiguity and personal risk
- Inclination to focus learning on meeting organizational needs
- Influence skills and the ability to use a variety of influence tactics
- Innovativeness and imagination
- Internal drive to make a difference
- Interpersonal communication skills that foster the ability to influence, lead, and manage

- Negotiation skills
- Openness to collaboration
- Open-mindedness
- Passion, conviction, and confidence in others
- Path-finding
- Political astuteness
- Problem-solving
- Professionalism
- Recognition of the challenge of change
- Recognition of the need for extensive innovation
- Resilience
- Respect for the process and content of change
- Responsibility, including personal responsibility for change management
- Self-monitoring
- Self-reliance
- Systemic change management
- Team effectiveness
- Technical expertise
- Tendency to question organizational assumptions
- Total commitment
- Transformational leadership behaviors
- Vision
- Willingness to listen and share

Drilling Down to Tell Stories About the Other Skills and Characteristics Employers Seek

While the ability to handle change is one of the most important skills about which to tell your stories in the job search, employers seek many other skills. Let's look at integrating skills beyond change skills into stories during the job search.

Questions for "Harvesting" Stories

Authors Karin Hurt and Dennis Metzger suggest that to "harvest" stories about skills, you should first brainstorm all the times you've successfully demonstrated a given skill. Then think about the related tasks that went into each example of the skill, asking such questions as these:

- What made the incident successful?
- Who were the main characters (such as boss, colleagues, subordinates, customers, or vendors) and what were they like?
- What is your role in the context of the story? (This question is important because job seekers often tell stories of successful team projects but neglect to clarify their own roles, thus failing to give themselves sufficient credit.)
- What specifically did the characters do?
- What stories emerge from each stage of the activity? What are the recurring themes common to the stories?
- How do the characters and plots differ in these stories?
- What lessons did you learn?

The authors also advise thinking about setting and plot, as well as the key message you want to convey about your skills and who your audience is. You may want to adjust your stories from employer to employer, for example, based on your knowledge of how each values a given skill. Hurt and Metzger further suggest identifying details that belong in each story, an idea that job-search training expert Dick Gaither echoes, recommending that job seekers consider such story details as where you were working, when the story took place, why you were involved in the story's central activity, how long it took, what the results were, and how the story demonstrates that you can add value for your next employer. Also ask yourself whether there was a defining moment in the incident you're describing and to what extent the incident was life-changing. Have your feelings about the incident changed over the years?

Bringing Stories to Life for Employers

Simmons recommends bringing your stories to life through sensory details, enabling whenever possible your audience to see, feel, hear, smell, and taste elements of your story. Drama, tension, and a description of transformation will engage readers and listeners in your story, writes Kerr Inkson in his book, *Understanding Careers*.

Consider, too, the needs of your audience as you choose stories to develop. In *All Marketers Are Liars*, Seth Godin advises that the worldview in the stories you tell must match the worldview of your audience—in this case, employers. Godin writes about story topics that always succeed with consumers. If you think of employers as consumers of the skills and experience that job seekers offer, you can apply some of the same topics to story development: shortcuts you've taken to make work more efficient, ways you've generated revenue, how you've made the workplace safer, and even how you've made work more fun. Godin also identifies ego as a successful story topic; consider opportunities to flatter an employer's ego by telling stories of your admiration for a company or your interviewer. Perhaps you've been a loyal user of the company's products for years. Or maybe you've seen a presentation your interviewer has given or read an article he or she has written.

Identifying and Communicating Important Skills

Story development is also an excellent technique for identifying the skills you most enjoy using. You might have some of the skills that employers most seek, but if you don't experience fulfillment from using them, you'll probably want to steer clear of jobs that emphasize those skills.

In the best-selling job-search book of all time, *What Color Is Your Parachute?* (a new edition of which is published annually), author Richard Bolles describes a "Seven Stories" exercise that not only prompts job seekers to develop stories about accomplishments, but also enables them to identify and prioritize their transferable skills. For each story, Bolles recommends identifying the goal you wanted to accomplish, a hurdle or obstacle that stood in the way, a step-by-step description of what you did to accomplish the goal, the outcome, a measure of the outcome (a way to quantify it, if possible), and the skills that you used to accomplish the goal. After creating seven of these stories, pick out the skills used and prioritize them based on how much you enjoyed using those skills.

Following is a compilation of skills and characteristics that experts say are most in demand by employers:

- Adaptability and transferability of skills (important for career changers)
- Administrative support
- Analytical thinking
- Areas of expertise
- Certification and/or degree(s)
- Communication
- Computer and technological proficiency
- Cost savings
- Creativity

- Customer/client service
- Consulting
- Entrepreneurial/startup skills
- Indicators of success/good performance/quality
- Interpersonal
- Languages
- Management/leadership/supervision
- Motivation
- Multicultural/cross-cultural/international
- Multitasking
- Organizational
- Problem-solving and troubleshooting
- Process improvement
- Quantitative skills
- Research, strategy, and planning
- Sales/marketing
- Team player who can also work independently
- Team player/team-builder
- Teaching/training
- Time management/ability to perform under deadline pressure
- Willingness to learn/ability to learn quickly
- Willingness to travel, relocate
- Work ethic/professionalism

More Examples of Stories That Illustrate Important Skills and Characteristics

Team Leadership

I found myself applying to my university because my cross-country coach told me not to. He advised me to take the free-ride cross-country scholarship to another school. I reasoned that academics and cross-country would be too much for me to handle there. So I applied to my current university because I felt I could compete comfortably while also excelling in my academics. My high-school coach was not too thrilled. He said, "You are making the biggest mistake of your life." He went on to tell me that the other college had a better cross-country department, and I would be running with a nationally ranked team. I challenged my coach and told him that with leadership and devotion, any team can be nationally ranked. Of course he laughed at my statement and restated that I was making a mistake.

Once I enrolled at my chosen school, I saw that my coach had been correct about the facilities and the character of the people on the team. The team members were not motivated, not athletic, and needless to say, lost every race they entered. Three other freshmen who had walked onto the team joined me in deciding to change the team members' attitudes. However, animosity was abundant between the upperclassmen and the freshmen. While we won races, the upperclassmen felt inferior, causing internal conflict in the team. Regardless, I was determined to persuade the team to mesh well to create unity. Consequently, the upperclassmen quit the team. Still, after winning our state title, we advanced to the national level, where we were expected to compete against the college my coach had wanted me to attend. We won the meet against that school, beating them out of a third-place medal. The moral of this story is that when I was challenged to do the impossible, my devotion, character, team leadership, and tenacity persevered, while also helping the team.

Goal-Setting

I grew up in a poor, broken home, yet decided that golf was my great passion in life. I creatively used my meager resources to buy golf clubs and later a junior membership for $180 at a local club. Every day for two years, I walked through the woods to the golf course where I would play, practice, and compete throughout high school. I eventually got a job at the club so I could buy myself a few necessities. I wanted to play in college but was nowhere near the player I needed to be to play or even get on the team. So over the summer before college, I worked on my golf game to the point where I won almost every tournament I entered. I spent every hour I had during the day to make myself a better all-around player. I eventually walked on my freshman year and was exempted from qualifying because I played so well in my first outing. Through the years my decision to play golf has influenced every part of my life 100 percent.

I didn't give up on a dream, and although I am not competing with Tiger, I realized all of the good decisions I made were based on the fact that I loved the game, but better yet, didn't give up on a goal.

Work Ethic

My stepfather was a role model and a strong influence in my life. He taught me about character; he taught me the tough lessons in life that some people learn too late or not at all. In one instance, he taught me the value of standing up for yourself. When the kids in his family (the "stepfamily") failed to accept me, he advised me that I would have to take the initiative to learn how to handle situations in which people passively exclude me—that I would have to do something that could get their attention. I soon learned to gather a couple of people and start up a card game or another fun activity to direct the focus on the activity instead of clashing personalities. I later realized that through this process, I had learned creative techniques to influence group dynamics.

In another situation, he taught me the value of hard work. After volunteering to do yard work one day, I got tired of the project after mowing the lawn. Hot, sweaty, and tired, I started to leave before the project was done, and he told me I couldn't leave. After several hours of pulling weeds, watering, weed-whacking, fertilizing, trimming, and prepping flower beds while my stepfather supervised from his comfortable lawn chair in the shade, I had learned that completing only a portion of a project is not acceptable when completion is expected; that there usually is a lot more work that goes on in the background of a finished product; that there will always be someone in that comfortable lawn chair watching others work—and that I wanted to be a supervisor in life.

Decision-Making

When I was a receptionist at a photography company, a man came in claiming to be the father of a student who was there to pick up the student's pictures. I asked him for identification, and he said that he had forgotten it. Normally, if the student is present with the parent and verifies that it is the correct parent, then we give the pictures to them. That wasn't the case here. There was no student. I refused to give him the pictures, and he became angry and left. Later that day, a different man came in to pick up those same pictures. This man had photo identification with him, and I told him about what had occurred earlier that day. He told me that his child was being stalked, and that the family had a restraining order against that man. I took the stalker's image from our security cameras and posted a picture behind the counter that indicated that he was not to have any contact with the pictures of that student. My decision-making skills helped prevent a dangerous situation because he has continued repeatedly to come into the store posing to other employees as the parent of that student.

Customer Service

As a customer service rep for a video-rental company, I once had an irate customer who left three messages on my voice mail in about 10 minutes demanding a call back. I contacted the customer, who was now even angrier because I had been in a meeting when her call came in. I listened to the customer explain that she was upset because she had purchased a loyalty program membership from us, and then several days later, we were giving away the same memberships at no cost. I apologized to the customer and asked her how I could help. She stated that she wanted her money back and she would no longer be a member. I agreed to refund her money. I then bought her a thank-you card and enclosed her refund and a free membership to our loyalty program. I also noticed that several times during the phone conversation, she had stopped to yell at her children, so I also enclosed two coupons for free kids' rentals. I thanked her for her business, apologized for not meeting her expectations, and invited her to bring her children in for a free video rental. I also enclosed my business card and asked her to call me directly if she was ever disappointed in any way while visiting one of our locations. She telephoned me when she received the card and told me that was the nicest thing any person had ever done for her when she was upset with a business. I again thanked her for her business and told her that she was my bread and butter. If she wasn't happy, then I couldn't be, either!

KSA (Knowledge, Skills, and Abilities) Statements

The KSA, an acronym for Knowledge, Skills, and Abilities, is a close cousin of the resume used primarily in government hiring. The KSA is another aspect of career-marketing communication in which storytelling can play a positive role. It's common to be asked to complete a KSA document, typically consisting of stories describing how you demonstrate three to six KSAs, for government jobs and sometimes for nongovernment positions, as well.

KSAs provide an opportunity to memorably elaborate on the skills that distinguish you from other candidates, and you can do so with stories. Jay Christensen, coauthor of *On-the-Job Communications for Business, the Professions, Government, and Industry,* encourages his business-communication students to write stories about career experiences that enabled them to achieve the knowledge, skill, or ability they are being asked to describe. With a KSA, you can develop a story, using the story-development frameworks in this chapter, to illustrate the knowledge, skill, or ability the employer requires you to demonstrate. The KSA, Christensen notes, "is the story of some part of the [job seeker's] work experience lifestyle." As with most stories used in job-search communication, KSAs should include results and quantification where possible.

Here are examples of partial KSA stories (a full KSA statement is about a page to a page and a half for each question asked).

Knowledge

Contracts: I have extensive experience with contracts and expertise in contract interpretation. The Salvation Army selected me to lead multimillion-dollar contract negotiations on corporate-wide benefits between the Salvation Army and healthcare providers. I also specialized in contract law during more than three years as an in-house attorney for SouthComm Communications,

Inc., where I reviewed, negotiated, and managed contracts. My contract interpretation skills are highly relevant to a Patent Attorney-Advisor's work because of their applicability to interpreting and analyzing statutes.

Skill

Skill in working independently on a wide variety of complex issues and making quick decisions with a high degree of accuracy at various stages of review simultaneously: I have great respect for the value of working independently without supervision to increase the productivity of the entire department and company. As a contract attorney, for example, I perform all work independently during each stage of document review. Law firms hire me with the understanding that they will not have to oversee my work because I produce quality output. They also depend on me to proficiently perform all assigned functions of my job with minimal supervision of staff attorneys and partners.

Ability

Ability to be organized and perform efficiently and proficiently in a fast-moving production environment under short deadlines: As an in-house attorney at SouthComm Communications, I excelled for more than three years in a fast-paced environment in which production against tight deadlines was critical and directly impacted the company's bottom-line sales and revenues. My job was to execute as many leases and other real-estate agreements as possible while limiting the company's exposure to risk. Cell sites could not be constructed to offload heavy-traffic areas without an executed lease, so the company depended on my organizational skills, proficiency, and rapid turnaround during contract negotiations. While speed was essential, I also succeeded in striking a balance between achieving business objectives and minimizing the company's liability.

Summary

You're armed with information about the skills you want to develop stories about and how to structure and frame your stories. You are now ready to consider how to apply your stories to your communications in various stages of your job search: networking, resumes, cover letters, portfolios, interview responses, and personal branding.

Part 2

Using Storytelling in Your Job Search

CHAPTER 3

Using Stories to Network with People

The often misunderstood art of networking is all about establishing relationships so that you can enlist support and comfortably ask for ideas, advice, and referrals to those with the power to hire you or advance your career. Storytelling provides a wonderful way to build these relationships because of its capability to instill emotional investment. Tell a good story to new network contacts you meet, and they will care much more about your success than if you had simply listed facts about yourself.

This chapter introduces two primary ways to integrate storytelling into your networking activities:

- Developing a brief introductory speech to succinctly tell network contacts who you are and what kind of work you seek. This speech is usually referred to as an "elevator speech," but for our purposes in this chapter, let's call it the Elevator Story. You can develop multiple versions of this story to have ready for various situations.
- Enlisting an "advisory board" of network contacts to review and critique the stories you use at all points in the job search.

The Elevator Speech Becomes the Elevator Story

By now the elevator speech is a fairly well-known tool not only for job seekers but also for organizations and individuals with products and services to sell. Authors of numerous Internet articles on the elevator speech offer speculations on the origin of the term—ranging from the notion that we often run into important people in elevators to the more common explanation that the elevator speech is a clear, concise bit of storytelling that can be delivered in the time it takes folks to ride from a building's top to the bottom in an elevator.

Whatever its exact origin, the Elevator Story is an exceptionally useful and versatile tool in numerous situations:

- Events designed specifically for networking.
- The casual networking opportunities we encounter nearly every day—the kids' soccer games, plane flights, waiting in line to buy tickets, and on and on.
- Career or job fairs.
- Cold calls to employers.
- Cold calls to absent employers: Rita Fisher of Career Change Resumes suggests that leaving your Elevator Story in the form of a voice-mail message virtually guarantees that the employer will call back. Hint: Assuming your story is sufficiently compelling, call after hours when you know for sure you will get the employer's voice mail.
- Opportunities within your own company to talk with higher-up honchos, let them know you're doing a great job, and position yourself for promotion.
- Job interviews, where the Elevator Story can provide the answer to at least two common interview queries: "Tell me about yourself" and "Why should I hire you?" (See chapter 7, "Interviews That Tell a Story.")

Experts vary widely as to the ideal length of an Elevator Story. Some experts say it should be as short as 15 seconds; others say it can be up to three minutes. There's no reason, however, that you can't employ both short and long versions. Different situations, after all, may well call for diverse approaches.

An Elevator Story is a story-based introduction of yourself used in situations where you are meeting a lot of people and probably not spending a great deal of time with any one of them. The trick is to make your introduction so intriguing—by using a story—that people will want to spend more time talking with you. You might also incorporate the speech into an initial phone conversation with a prospective new member of your network.

Structure and Examples

At its most basic level, the Elevator Story's structure is this:

> *Hi, my name is ___________. I'm in the _______________ field, and I'm looking to _____________________.*

The last blank would be filled in with your current career aspiration, whether it is to stay within your field and move up or move into a different career.

Here's a slightly more embellished example:

Greetings. My name is Indra Ghee. I'm an accomplished, published, senior-level scientist with 12 years of experience in molecular biology.

A college student or new graduate might add the following to the basic structure:

Hi, my name is ____________. I will be graduating/I just graduated from ______________________ with a degree in ______________________. I'm looking to ______________________.

These bare-bones structures don't tell much of a story, though, and are not terribly memorable, so consider adding meat to the bones of your Elevator Story with additional details about your background and what you can offer, as in these examples:

Hi, I'm Joe Fredericks. I'm a versatile project/program management executive with 15-plus years of leadership and business management expertise gained from positions of increasing responsibility in both the U.S. Navy and the private sector. I recently reduced my employer's costs by 35 percent through leading a hardware and software redesign of the access control system, which also resulted in improved performance, increased reliability, and additional features.

I'm Valerie Obermarle, a creative, outside-the-box thinker who approaches strategic development with innovative vision, high ethical standards, unsurpassed work ethic, and ability to communicate effectively across management levels and disciplines to build highly effective cross-functional teams.

Hello, I'm Jim Swing, a brand-new MBA and an accounting professional with three years of hands-on experience in multiple aspects of accounting operations.

Hi there, I'm Tim Tejera, but you can call me a technically proficient, enthusiastic new computer-science graduate who possesses comprehensive, practical knowledge of the latest hardware and programming technologies along with expertise in multiple software applications. I might look like a college kid, but I accelerated time-to-market for embedded software by 25 percent by using appropriate software quality tools, improved debugging methods, and timely personnel training.

I'm Janet Singleton. I like to think of myself as an accomplished organizational-development professional with more than a decade of experience in project leadership, needs assessment/definition, resource identification, and process/change facilitation. I took the initiative to improve medical benefits and develop systems for handling benefits-enrollment data after being recruited initially to set up an HR department for a company that has grown from 8 to 25 employees.

Hello, I'm Cynthia Bee. I'm a licensed industrial engineering professional with eight years of experience in medical diagnostic manufacturing and personal products manufacturing and an additional five years of experience in logistics.

Hi, Jack Burnham here. As a diligent, quantitatively skilled achiever, I'm equipped, through my master's-level training in taxation, to play a key role in your organization's tax research, analysis, and planning. I also have expertise in interpreting tax code, regulations, revenue rulings, and case law, as well as preparing tax returns for corporations, partnerships, individuals, estates, and trusts.

Hi, I'm Jenny Swade. I'd like to use my newly minted MBA-education to apply organizational-development theory and practice at a growing firm. I can particularly contribute strong analytical, quantitative, research, and planning skills, along with solid leadership, interpersonal, and people-management capabilities. I enhanced my company's pricing competitiveness by assessing and selecting vendors for new systems.

Hello, my name is Andy Fellows. I'm an entrepreneurial marketing professional with more than 15 years of uncompromising accomplishments in multiple facets of building, marketing, and operating highly successful academic product sales businesses. I attained a 170 percent increase in 12 months by expanding the academic market for software through direct sales to universities worldwide, channel partners, and publishers, as well as by implementing solid prospecting strategies to cultivate new business opportunities and broaden the customer base.

Hi, I'm Kimberly Jackson. I'm a customer-service professional with a solid background in administrative management and technology support as well as experience in public relations for internal and external clients, team-building, technology training, quality assurance, contract negotiation, and event planning.

Hello, I am Ed Kendall. As an international marketing consultant, I realized more than a 50 percent increase in overall profitability and $500,000 in new revenue through directing Euro conversion in four countries while simultaneously improving client relationships and controlling project costs.

Hi, I'm Sandra Dinkleman. You might be interested in knowing that I recently stabilized a highly chaotic operational and customer-service situation by taking control and implementing new heightened customer-service standards and collaborating with staff members to improve the company image and boost the morale of my employer's staff.

Hooking Your Network Contacts into Your Story

You could stick with a fairly basic structure and a simple Elevator Story and see where it takes you. Or you can begin your story with a conversational teaser or "hook." If you add this element of intrigue—a story—the ensuing conversation has even more potential. Look, for example, at how a conversation might go that starts with an intriguing story:

> **Networker #1:** Hi, my name is Tom Jacobsen. I was born a lucky Arkansan.
>
> **Networker #2:** How so?
>
> **Networker #1:** Because I was born on July 11th, 7-11. I have been fortunate enough to meet two presidents, Reagan and Clinton, and the richest man in the world, the late Sam Walton. I am also blessed to be part of a good family with one brother and three sisters. This family has instilled in me strong values, which were reinforced by volunteer work in my church and community. Trustworthiness and honesty are my defining characteristics. Quiet by nature, I am the "strong, silent type." Far from boring, I have a great sense of humor, and I even own a goose. I intend to achieve my goals through hard work.

Take a look at another example:

> **Networker #1:** Hi, my name is Aleksandra Auersperg. I propagate teamwork and believe that brain share is key to success.
>
> **Networker #2:** What does that mean?
>
> **Networker #1:** I thrive on the synergy created by a team working well together, sharing, encouraging, and supporting each other. For example, back home in Slovenia, teamwork was everything—a value that is basic to life. All my previous work has been in a team-driven work environment. I very much believe that two ideas are better than one, and two people will attain much more than one individual person.

And one more:

> **Networker #1:** Hi, my name is Barney Joiner. You might think I'm a pimp, but I'm not.
>
> **Networker #2:** That's good to know.

Networker #1: I have the PMP credential—which can be pronounced "pimp"—but it's actually Project Management Professional. I'm results-driven and offer a master's-level education and a proven track record in project leadership, product development, project initiation and execution, and exceptional client management.

The concern with an intriguing story, of course, is that you'll sound corny or hokey. And, in fact, chances are you will. I'll admit that when I first researched these Elevator Stories, I found them very corny. But they work—by hooking your conversation partner into learning more about you.

Requesting Action

Even the most intriguing Elevator Stories often lack an important element: a request for action. Here are some action items that you can add to the end of your Elevator Story in various situations:

At a career fair: *"I'd like to take your business card, as well as leave my networking card and resume. Would it be possible for me to get a spot on your company's interview schedule?"*

In a networking situation: *"What advice do you have for me? Can you suggest any employers I should be contacting?"*

Cold-calling an employer: *"When can we set up a meeting to discuss how I can help your company?"*

Telephone or e-mail situations: *"May I send you my resume?" (For in-person situations, you should always have resumes handy.) If your resume resides in electronic form on the Internet, you can say: "May I refer you to my resume on the Web at [insert Web address here]?"*

The Expanded Elevator Story

You can expand on your Elevator Story in networking situations in which you have more time to talk about yourself, such as when you are visiting the office of a prospective member of your network or having lunch with a contact. It's also an effective response when you're conducting an informational interview, and the interviewee turns the tables and starts asking questions about you. This longer version is typically one to three minutes long and contains more about your background, qualifications, and skills.

Obviously, you don't want your expanded Elevator Story to sound memorized. But you are, after all, talking about yourself, so the material is not hard to remember. It helps to write it out first—outline form is fine—then read it over a few times and practice saying it without reading or memorizing it. Practice it in front of friends and members of your network, too. It's not a big deal if you forget a detail as long as you remember the main points you want to get across.

Here are some samples, which range from about 300 to 400 words. Remember that the point of composing such stories is not for them to sound exactly the way they are written. But writing them will help imprint them on your brain so that you can tell them with the natural ease of a storyteller.

My desire to become a businesswoman began at a young age. I can clearly remember many summers of my childhood, the kind of summers that couldn't come quickly enough and that seemed to last an eternity. I would set up shop in front of my house, ready to sell lemonade to the neighbors or the occasional UPS man. A colorful sign and decorated table would adorn my roadside booth to entice customers. After a while, I became bored with just the lemonade shop. I wanted to draw in my peers, so I began to collect Happy Meal toys during the year. When summer came, I would fill up my red wagon and tug it along to the shop to sell nifty gadgets and toys in addition to the lemonade.

Eager for a change and the excitement of something new, I passed along the lemonade shop to my younger sisters and decided to move onto other avenues. My best friend Ashley and I opened up "Maggie and Ashley's Place"—another business endeavor, this one providing jewelry services. We bought bead boxes and filled them to the brim with multicolored thread and an assortment of beads. On the inside cover of our boxes, we had a log to record orders, determine the price based on the thread and number of beads used, and provide an estimate as to when the orders would be completed. We also started to use the computer technology that we learned about in school to design and print our own business cards.

Looking back, I'm amazed at the precision, quality, and detail I gave to these businesses, attributes I continue to strive for to this day. From brainstorming ideas and seeing them through to fruition, I found excitement and vigor in pursuing my dreams. Over the years I've learned to never give up and if something isn't working out, to forge a new path to make it my own. I truly admire Eleanor Roosevelt for saying that "the future belongs to those who believe in the beauty of their dreams," and I plan to see to it that I never stop dreaming of bigger and better aspirations.

I started playing fastpitch softball when I was 10 years old. I have missed a ball in the field, struck out at the plate, and even been injured during a game. However, I love softball unconditionally because I have discovered elements of my life that I truly treasure from simply playing the game. I have learned the importance of being a team player as well as communicating effectively to execute the game plan. I have established leadership qualities by leading by example and motivating others to be the best that they can be. Most importantly, softball has taught me that only dedication and devotion toward your goals brings success; therefore, hard work and patience are the keys to being successful.

Because the preceding stories have their roots in childhood, they are especially heartwarming and emotional. But of course, most Elevator Stories will come from professional experience, as in these examples:

I have worked with my father in our family business since well before I turned 18. My father and I own a company that specializes in diverse business fields, primarily property development and hydro-engineering. We branched into hydro-engineering mainly because I had such a fascination with renewable energy. I expressed this interest to my father and our team of engineers, and I was given the "greenlight" to set up a company and do some research. After two years, our company obtained all necessary approvals from the government, and our first mini-hydro project was on the way. Sri Lanka has two monsoon seasons and a central region of mountains, which is the perfect recipe for generating hydro-electricity. The project began operation in September 2007, and it has become one of the most profitable subsidiaries in our establishment. The confidence and the experience that I've gained provide me with strength and guidance for my future endeavors.

My determination and ability to connect people with resources that produce results is my greatest attribute. For example, my first retail management position involved an independently owned startup pet store in Sausalito. My goal was to establish a profitable business within a two-year time frame. I hired and developed a knowledgeable and trained team of employees, researched the market to properly merchandise the store, connected with the community to make it an enjoyable shopping experience and develop loyal customers, and initiated procedures to manage expenses, shrink, and inventory. The result was a well-established community pet store that grew into a $1.25 million a year business. I also have a strong sense of equality and thrive on the experience of learning from and leading a team. I enjoy setting goals and empowering others to achieve their goals. I am fearless and persistent when it comes to connecting with the people who can make a difference and asking them for what we need to complete a task. I have excellent communication skills and a keen eye when it comes to grasping the big picture and finding those who will contribute their talents to creating success.

Enlisting Your Personal Advisory Board in Reviewing and Critiquing Your Job Search Stories

One of the most effective uses of networking is the potential to build an inner circle of close advisers who can guide and support you through your job search. They're the ones that you can always feel comfortable calling on for advice, the ones who will conduct practice interviews with you, and the folks who can review and critique the stories you develop for all phases of the job search. They can help you develop and tell your stories. Ask for feedback from them about your strengths and weaknesses, and build stories around your strengths as perceived by those who know you best.

Test your stories on your close inner circle. Ask them to place themselves in the employer's mindset as they listen to or read your stories, and request that they react as an employer would react. You can then use their feedback to refine and polish your stories.

Writing on Business Week Online, Liz Ryan, founder and CEO of WorldWIT (Women. Insight. Technology.), recommends trading resumes with colleagues and asking the reader to "look for the story that comes through."

Expand your network by conducting informational interviews, which are informal meetings with people in your industry. You can use informational interviews to learn more about jobs and make connections—but not to ask for a job. Learn about industry trends through these interviews so that you can tailor your stories to what's happening in your field. Ask interviewees what the top people in your field offer that others don't, and then incorporate your matching qualities into your stories.

Story Formula Roundup from the Experts

The following roundup of formulas suggested by experts should provide food for thought for the structure that works best for you in planning and outlining your Elevator Story. Remember that in a job-hunting situation, the listener's tacit question may be "Why should I (or any employer) hire you?"

You'll notice that one thing nearly all the experts have in common is their emphasis on stressing your benefit to the listener and touching on how you're better than the competition. This principle encompasses many names—such as Unique Selling Proposition, value proposition, benefit statement, competitive advantage, deliverables, and differentiation—but the bottom line is the same. What can you bring to the employer, and how can you do it better than anyone else? Telling a story is a great way to answer those questions.

Tony Jeary

This framework for planning your Elevator Story is adapted from Tony Jeary, author of *Life Is a Series of Presentations:*

1. Define your audience universe.
2. Define the content or subject matter of your story.
3. Define your objective.
4. Define your desired image or style.
5. Define your key message and build your story around it.

Marisa D'Vari

Author, speaker, and consultant Marisa D'Vari suggests starting the Elevator Story process by writing down three key points about your product (you, in this case) and telling stories about how these points will benefit an employer.

Jean Hanson

Here's a story-based variation on a formula suggested by Certified Professional Virtual Assistant Jean Hanson:

1. Who am I? (Introduce yourself.)
2. What field or industry am I in?
3. What position am I in and what position do I want to be in? In what capacity do I serve or want to serve?
4. What is my USP (Unique Selling Proposition)? What makes me different from the competition?
5. A brief story that illustrates the benefits that employers can derive from my skills, based on my proven accomplishments.

Example:

1. Who am I?

   Hi, I'm Thad VanIderstine.

2. What field or industry am I in?

   I'm a strategic operations executive in the cable-TV sector.

3. What position am I in and what position do I want to be in? In what capacity do I serve or want to serve?

   I want to add value to an organization in a senior position by being involved in many facets of operations and how strategy translates into increasing the bottom line.

4. What is my USP (Unique Selling Proposition)? What makes me different from the competition?

   A successful manager must be able to provide valuable feedback in a timely fashion while allowing employees to be independent and coaching them on both their strengths and opportunities for development. I've been a successful manager because I lead by example.

5. A brief story that illustrates the benefits that employers can derive from my skills, based on my proven accomplishments.

   For instance, when I was asked to manage a field project, one team was struggling to get the program off the ground. One of the issues they had was the ability to effectively manage outsourcing. So I showed them how to take charge of meetings with the outsource vendors, meet less frequently, and ensure that everyone was accountable. The result was the successful management of the program, and the respect that I gained from the team, rather than potential resentment for my taking over the project. Senior management recognized the entire team for launching the program.

Randy Dipner

Next is a formula that requires researching targeted employers and telling your Elevator Story to someone connected to the targeted employer. It's adapted from Randy W. Dipner of Meeting the Challenge, Inc.:

1. List target employers. Group them and ultimately define the employer.
2. Define the need or opportunity. That is, what critical issue does the employer face?
3. Identify yourself in terms of a job function or contribution. What do you do?
4. Tell a story that incorporates the benefits—not the features—that you provide to the employer. Prioritize the benefits to identify the single benefit that is the most compelling reason for the employer to hire you. To the maximum extent possible, the benefit should be both quantified and expressed in story form.

5. Develop a statement of the primary differentiation of yourself, which should be the single most important thing that sets you apart from the competition.

Example:

1. Define the employer.

   I'm looking to join an organization—like Tornado Marketing—that values an impact player who can help maximize brand productivity. My ideal job would allow me to interact with all areas of the company in all marketing-communications disciplines, from market research, to agency management, to sales and marketing.

2. Define the need or opportunity. That is, what critical issue does the employer face?

   Based on my research, I know that Tornado has a major new client that is looking to raise its visibility and build its brand in the banking sector.

3. Identify yourself in terms of a job function or contribution. What do you do?

   I go far beyond advertising, delving into internal communications, sales discussions, and virtually any client interaction. Throughout my career, I've continually progressed to take on more responsibility because of my commitment to ensuring the integrity of marketing and collaborating with all areas of the organization.

4. Tell a story that incorporates the benefits—not the features—that you provide to the employer.

   One of the things I am most proud of is the awards program I created to help a former bank client become better known for catering to small businesses and recognizing their contributions to the economy. I managed all aspects of the program, including communications, securing an independent judging panel, instituting an impartial judging process, and overseeing public-relations strategy and tactics. I created a media strategy around the program and winner announcement in local markets. The program generated 2 million media impressions in the first year and experienced an increased response of 25 percent in the second year while reducing the budget by more than 30 percent. And internally I then used the results of this program to create a brand-new look and feel for the bank's marketing communications. I was recruited for this opportunity because of my successful management of the Leadership Awards program.

5. Develop a statement of the primary differentiation of yourself, which should be the single most important thing that sets you apart from the competition.

   While my specialty is brand-building, I'm the complete package. I help clients increase awareness, favorability, and ultimately sales by employing a variety of marketing communications disciplines, including market research, program development and management, advertising, and public relations. I've been successful in my career because I'm passionate about what I do, extremely energetic, and have the ability to be both strategic and tactical.

Pepperdine University's Graziadio School of Business and Management

The business school at Pepperdine University suggests knowing your audience and knowing yourself, including key strengths, adjectives that describe you, what you are trying to let others know about you, and a statement of your interest in the company or industry the person represents. Armed with that knowledge, you can then outline the Elevator Story using these questions:

1. Who am I?
2. What do I offer?
3. What problems can I solve?
4. What are the main contributions I can make?
5. What should the listener do as a result of hearing this?

Example:

1. Who am I?

   I am an experienced financial operations manager with more than 15 years of managerial experience and a track record of leading teams of people who achieve benchmark results. I have an extensive background in operations analysis, training, and managing the performance metrics in an operations environment.

2. What do I offer?

   I offer excellent project-management skills, and I'm a pro at cost savings.

3. What problems can I solve?

   I can implement money-saving projects. I led a project team that came up with new payment programs for people experiencing serious long-term hardships that *were impacting their ability to make regular payments on their debts. I suggested the project to the president of our company. My project team designed the requirements for the new programs and the system requirements to support the enrollments. We determined the metrics needed to measure the program's success, helped design the required training for the program at inception, and handled the actual rollout. Within 12 months, we had saved more than $50 million in potential losses through the use of the new programs.*

4. What are the main contributions I can make?

   My background demonstrates a strong record of loyalty to my employers as well as top results and consistent promotions to positions of increasing responsibility. I can contribute strong analytical, communication, and leadership skills, and can build a strong team of people focused on achieving the organization's goals.

5. What should the listener do as a result of hearing this?

   Can you suggest any employers who could benefit from my skills and experience?

Summary

Stories are a natural in networking. The Elevator Story is an effective cousin to the Elevator Speech that is commonly used in introductions to prospective network contacts. You'll find various opportunities while you are networking to expand on your Elevator Story. Your network contacts can help you identify the story-worthy skills and traits you possess, as well as provide excellent sounding boards for your job search stories.

CHAPTER 4

Telling Stories on Your Resume

The contemporary resume, with its bullet points and terse, clipped phrases, seems like the complete opposite of any type of storytelling device. Some players in the hiring process, particularly recruiters, tend to want candidates to stick to the facts in their resumes. Others, however, especially those who make direct hiring decisions, appreciate a resume that opens a window to your personality through storytelling.

"Your resume should be about…telling stories that register," writes Seth Godin in *All Marketers Are Liars*. In his 2002 book, *Making Stories: A Practical Guide for Organizational Leaders and Human Resource Specialists*, Terrence Gargiulo points out that human-resource managers prepare to interview candidates by reading resumes with their "story mind." Putting himself into the mindset of HR people, he envisions using the information in the resume to "construct a story and image of the person." As a job seeker, you can help the hiring decision-maker by crafting a narrative that grabs the reader.

When read by human eyes, your resume will get the reader's attention for only 2.5 to 20 seconds. In his popular book about intuition, *Blink!*, Malcolm Gladwell talks about "thin-slicing," which he defines as "the ability of our unconscious to find patterns in situations and behavior based on very narrow slices of experience." Employers can be said to "thin-slice" when they glance at a resume. Rare is the employer who will read even close to the entire resume on the first pass. Yet they will usually put your resume into a "yes," "no," or "maybe" pile based on the tiny slice of your resume that actually catches their attention. That's why compelling narrative can be key to intriguing your reader. The usual thin slices of your experience served up in a resume don't enable you to weave a theme to resonate with the employer.

Attention-Getting Online Story Resumes

Two hilarious examples of story resumes appear on the Internet. One is a musical, animated creation that attracted a great deal of notice and was actually a fairly serious attempt to obtain a job. It appears at www.paradoxware.com/alstudio/cv/en.htm. Another, from Allen Williams, at www.itsallaboutallen.com/navigation/section2/mainpage.html, would seem to be a quite tongue-in-cheek incarnation of a resume.

"Too long and boring" comprise two of the top complaints about most resumes voiced by Liz Ryan of WorldWIT. Contributing to a blog called "Get That Job!" Ryan cites one of her favorite resumes—from a controller who includes this telling line on his resume: "Unusually wicked sense of humor for a Finance type." Ryan notes that "the human need for stories should be a vital clue to job hunters, whose resumes often have as much dramatic punch as the back of a cereal box. Your resume is your marketing brochure. It has to tell your story." She suggests reading through your resume with the fresh eyes of an employer who will wonder, "Who is this person?"

An unnamed blogger on the blog Fincareer similarly writes that "by highlighting and interpreting experiences in light of the job or career alternative you are contemplating, your story will get the quality and coherence needed to win a recruiter's trust and interest." With a storied resume, you can often explain the rationale and value of what you've done.

Just as valuable as the resume itself is the process of compiling it, write Herminia Ibarra and Kent Lineback in *Harvard Business Review,* because "it entails drafting your story." The authors advise that "everything in the resume must point to one goal—which is, of course, the climax of the story you're telling." They cite a job seeker who better defined what excited her about her chosen field every time she wrote her story in a piece of job search communication.

Most employers also want to see substantiation of your claims about yourself, which is something you can accomplish through storytelling. Too many resumes are collections of adjectives and meaningless puffery with no stories to back up their claims. In focus-group research conducted for this book, participants found a story-based resume (the Wesley Edwards resume shown on page 74) more memorable than one that did not contain story, noting that the storytelling resume "leaves more of an impression."

Guidelines for Creating a Story-Based Resume

The resume is the trickiest component in career-marketing communication in which to tell stories. Here are some guidelines to keep in mind when creating a story-based resume:

- **Use an introductory profile.** A commonly used section at the top of the resume, a Qualifications Summary or Professional Profile, provides an excellent vehicle for telling the story of who you are professionally. Later in this chapter you'll see how.
- **Go light on job duties.** KPMG Principal Mary Anne Davidson observed on the HR.com Web site, "Candidates write about what their positions entailed and not what they actually did. So they tell us their job was to do XYZ. I know what controllers do. I know what recruiters do. I need to know what accomplishments you made in your role. This makes you different than another candidate." Susan Britton Whitcomb, author of *Résumé Magic,* one of the most highly recommended resume books on the market, calls accomplishments "the linchpin of a great resume." Her chapter on accomplishments is one of the best resources to help you compose effective accomplishments stories.
- **Stress accomplishments.** To a great extent, if a job activity cannot be portrayed as an accomplishment, it may not be worthy of mention in your resume. Thus, your resume should be primarily accomplishments-driven (rather than driven by duties and responsibilities), and accomplishments are best communicated in story form. Think about what would have been different in each situation without your actions? What would not have happened if you hadn't been there? How did you leave each organization better than you found it?
- **Lead with the results.** Accomplishment stories should include the situation, problem, or challenge that contextualizes your achievement, the action you took, and the results you attained; however, you should tell this story in reverse order—results, action, problem/situation/challenge. Why? Because, as I noted earlier, the employer looks at your resume so quickly. Results need to be listed first for each accomplishment so that these outcomes catch the reader's eye. So, instead of SAR, PAR, or CAR stories (see pages 19–20), you'll tell RAS, RAP, or RAC stories. You'll see more information and examples later in this chapter.
- **Save the stories for the addendum.** Some professional resume writers use the tactic of going easy on the story approach in the resume itself, but letting loose with stories of accomplishments, results, and outcomes in a resume addendum or career biography. Addendum examples appear later in this chapter.

- **Tell concise stories.** Most employers prefer a resume that is formatted mostly in bullet points—which don't exactly lend themselves to storytelling. You can tell stories in resume bullet points, but they must be concise, not wordy. Think of a story-based resume as "story lite." You can go into more detail in a resume addendum, in your cover letter, and later in your interview. Focus-group participants emphasized the conciseness point repeatedly, strongly cautioning against wordiness, overblown adjectives, too much information, and the impact of accomplishments lost in a sea of text. One participant said, "If you could combine the brevity of [the nonstorytelling resume] with the...details of [the story-based resume], that would be the preferred ideal."
- **Humanize and personalize your resume.** The trend in resumes has been to eschew personal information and interests. But this type of human-interest information can work for you as long as you relate it to professional skills. It also helps to reveal more of your story to the employer and portrays you as someone he or she would like to get to know better. For their book, *Insider's Guide to Finding a Job*, Shelly Goldman and Wendy Enelow interviewed 66 top corporate human-resources executives, recruiters, hiring managers, and career experts, among them Bill Welsh of Equinox Fitness, who believes that personal information on a resume is important and that "the more he knows about someone, the more informed his hiring decision will be." Revelation of personal interests and affiliations can indicate cultural fit with the prospective employer, create a bond with an interviewer with similar interests, and demonstrate transferable and applicable skills. For example, the following sample bullet point shows how a job seeker might apply a slice of personal life to the corporate culture of the targeted employer.
    - Avid outdoor enthusiast poised to contribute my passion for outdoor sports to your firm's mission to promote the active lifestyle.
- **Know what to leave out.** It's wise to be story-minded when composing your resume so that you know what to leave out. A resume is neither a job application nor a life history. It's a marketing document, so it need not and should not be all-inclusive. Keeping your story—and better yet, your branded story (see chapter 8)—in mind as you craft your resume can help you judiciously omit material that, in the words of David W. Brown, author of *Organization Smarts,* "doesn't advance [your] personal narrative." WorldWIT's Ryan similarly notes that most resumes "tell us what we don't need to know, for instance, the typical tasks in a Marketing Research Manager's job." She goes on to describe how most

resumes read: "I did this job. I stopped that. I had these responsibilities." Job seekers need to dig deeper, Ryan exhorts. "What was your motivation?" she asks. "Surely you didn't go through these experiences in a daze. What was going on during that time? You've built your career, thus far, from scratch. How and why?"

- **Tailor your resume to each job you seek.** Remember that you don't have to tell the same stories on every resume you send out. The ideal scenario is to tailor your resume for every position you apply for so that you can change up your stories, selecting those that are most appropriate for the job at hand.
- **Quantify.** Employers love numbers. Atlanta-based resume writer Gayle Oliver refers to these numbers as "performance metrics," for example:
    - Increased sales by 50% over the previous year.
    - Generated total meal sales 20% higher than those of the other servers in the restaurant.
    - Supervised staff of 25.
    - Served a customer base of 150, the largest on firm's customer-service team.
- **Use superlatives.** As Donald Asher notes in his excellent resume reference for college students, *From College to Career,* you can impress employers with words such as "first," "only," "best," "most," and "highest." Look for details that distinguish your accomplishments. For example, career author Rob Sullivan suggests that if you won an award, tell how many people were eligible for the award. It sounds more impressive to say, for example, that you were selected for the award from 300 candidates than it would to simply say you won the award. Try to identify what made your achievement special, Sullivan urges.
- **Define success.** Think about the critical success factors for the type of position you are targeting, advises Oliver. Tell a story of what it looks like to succeed in this kind of position. Brainstorm stories of how past employers defined you as successful.

Using a Professional Profile or Qualifications Summary Section to Tell the Story of Who You Are

Twenty years ago or so, a Profile or Qualifications Summary section was somewhat unusual on a resume. Career experts trace the use of summaries and profiles, which include information about candidates' qualities beyond their credentials, to the publication of the late Yana Parker's *The Damn Good Resume Guide* in 1983. Today these sections are seen as an important resume element, consisting of four or five bullet points that encapsulate your top selling points.

So, a typical Profile or Summary section might consist of these items:

- Bullet point summarizing your professional identity in a nutshell. Tells the story of who you are.
- Bullet point addressing interpersonal communication skills and optionally including any applicable language skills. Tells the story of how well you communicate.
- One or more bullet points addressing key job-specific skills, ideally supported by stories, quotes from employers, or quantification.
- A bullet point addressing computer/technical skills.
- Optional bullet points addressing relocation, willingness to travel, work eligibility, or other contingencies, if applicable.

Some employers say they don't like Summary/Profile sections because they are full of unsubstantiated fluff. Therefore, it's incumbent upon you to substantiate as much of the Summary/Profile section as possible—with stories, as well as with numbers, examples, and quotes from those who know your work. Any bullet points that are not substantiated in the Summary/Profile section itself should be substantiated later in the resume.

Sample Bullet Points

Here are examples of story-substantiated bullet points:

- Demonstrated organizational skills at the highest level; successfully completed all assignments, meeting all goals and timelines from initiating complex and sensitive operations in the United States and abroad to establishing overseas office.
- Successfully deployed unsurpassed interpersonal skills during professional interactions with U.S. government personnel, representatives of Fortune 500 defense-industry corporations, and as an instructor/lecturer for business groups and government employees.
- Innovative decision-maker who consistently made informed purchasing choices on ERP and other software packages by developing fully operational, user-configurable, corporate intranet, and numerous in-house custom-built, Oracle-based applications.

- Accomplished facilitator with reputation for highly effective team-building skills proven through overcoming team resistance and collaboratively completing key intranet project well before four-month deadline.
- Enthusiastic self-starter who addressed seemingly insurmountable technical difficulties in software program that threatened timely document submission to the FDA; research efforts resulted in software upgrade that enabled swift completion of time-sensitive documents.
- Solutions-oriented manager who overcame negativity of two unsuccessful prior project attempts by applying specialized project-management methodology and design techniques.

Targeting the First Bullet Point

Begin your Summary/Profile section with a bullet point that tells the story of your professional identity in a nutshell. It's the most important bullet point because it puts you into focus, characterizes who you are, and tells the story of what you can contribute. If the reader should happen to read no further in your Summary/Profile section, he or she should at least have a sense of your essence from this first bullet point.

Examples:

- Dynamic MBA-level professional with more than seven years of experience in successful leadership of business and organizational turnarounds that involve multiple, complex dynamics and cross disciplines and management levels.
- Ph.D.-level leader, change agent, and social activist who has developed broad range of programs and procedures that yielded cost effectiveness and maximum utilization of resources and accountability.
- Dynamic performer with background of achievement and success in entrepreneurial and business-development roles that have catapulted bottom-line revenues.
- Multi-faceted change agent with significant human-resources experience who applies expertise in cross-functional process improvement to achieve meaningful organizational change.
- Entrepreneurial, outside-the-box, critical thinker with strong quantitative and research skills, functional IT skillset, and enthusiasm to deliver on front-line globalization issues.
- Goal-driven achiever with strong organization skills who performs as both versatile individual and team player with ability to quickly assess,

(continued)

(continued)

comprehend, and manage customer relations while upholding company values.

- Accomplished project-management professional with more than 15 years of experience in capably and creatively delivering operating solutions through proficiencies in business analysis, problem-solving, process improvement, and software development.
- Self-motivated professional with strong financial skills who expertly manages multiple deadlined tasks, including accurate processing and reporting accounts payable/receivable, reconciliations, and payroll.
- Outgoing customer-service professional known for outstanding interpersonal, organizational, and prioritization skills, as well as people-management know-how that consistently elicits positive interaction with internal and external clientele.
- Highly motivated sales professional with excellent communications and presentation skills as well as a reputation for instantly developing rapport that produces immediate sales results while paving the way for future sales successes.
- Goal-driven IT operations and technical-support management professional with 15+ years of experience and commitment to delivering high-quality technical service and support to multiple IT customers concurrently.
- Master's-level professional known for strong analytical and quantitative skills and applying sound research methodologies to assess needs, identify alternatives, and recommend strategies that facilitate optimal healthcare outcomes.
- Dedicated health and education professional who is uniquely qualified to deliver outside-the-box accomplishments in pharmaceutical sales through exceptional ability to synthesize and disseminate product knowledge and contribute immediately to your bottom line.
- Efficiency-driven call-center professional who upholds highest accuracy performance standards and operational effectiveness through genuine talent for motivational, interpersonal teaching and mentoring.
- Accomplished accounting professional and licensed CPA with extensive experience in developing and implementing highly efficient accounting systems that deliver accurate reporting and ensure compliance with established control policies and procedures.
- Accomplished QA professional with 15+ years of progressive experience and proven record of significant, successful contribution in wide range of organizations that previously had no quality standards or programs in place.

- Dynamic B2B/B2C technology marketing executive with exemplary career record of bringing products to market, precisely targeting consumer demographic while maximizing adoption and profitability.
- Conscientious direct caregiver who provides meticulous, fully attentive, individualized nursing care to meet complex array of patient needs by employing nursing process methodology including assessment, planning, implementation, and evaluation.
- Dynamic professional with strong commitment to women's sports and proven track record as both competitor and event organizer.
- Highly proficient, multifaceted professional with demonstrated ability to identify and define needs, formulate solutions, direct and supervise multiple participants, and capably juggle and effectively manage several priorities simultaneously.

Give the Bulleted Items Parallel Structure

An important technique to enable your reader to interpret your Summary/Profile section as a story is to make it parallel, as though each bullet point is completing the same sentence. This kind of narrative flow helps readability enormously. Imagine that each Summary/Profile bullet point answers the question, "Who are you, and what can you do for our organization?" and finishes an unstated but understood sentence that begins: "I am a(n)...."

Let's see how this formula works in practice:

- [I am a] Seasoned systems analyst with strong commitment to time and resource budgets, new-business development, strategic planning, innovation, technology trends, customer-service needs, and close collaboration with sales and marketing during development.
- [I am a] Competent problem-solver who resolved sales and shipping issues by creating internal customer-care system and saving 20% on shipping; researched and delivered Web conferencing service for sales that saved 30% of travel budgets.
- [I am a] Visionary innovator who partnered with another programmer to create pioneering language-learning software that earned national attention; served as lead analyst for revolutionary legal document generating and tracking product.

(continued)

(continued)

- [I am a] Technical guru who provided direct support for successful million-dollar negotiation with major print vendor and completed many successful major conversions from mainframe to mini-computer systems.
- [I am a] Strong communicator who was voted best specification writer—with least number of rewrites—by programmers and their managers.

You'll note that the story-based grammatical structure of these parallel bullet points goes like this:

- [Adjective] [noun] [connecting words] [phrase describing skill/strength/expertise] [supported by quote, example, numbers]

Composing Accomplishments Bullet Points

As you list each job on your resume, you will likely want to use bullet points (which employers prefer over paragraph form) describing what you did—and more importantly, what you accomplished and what results you attained—under each job title. Presenting your accomplishments in your resume represents a case where it's okay, indeed desirable, to give away the end of the story first. Tell the Result (R) of your Action (A) first so that it catches the employer's attention. Then, ideally, describe the Situation (S), Problem (P), or Challenge (C) that your Action addressed. Quantify wherever possible.

Note in these examples from diverse resumes that, because of resume space limitations and employers' preference for conciseness, the Situation, Problem, or Challenge is not always described:

- Produced sales growth from $50K in backlog to more than $31 million in backlog in three years by building high-performance, multifunctional/multidiscipline sales team comprising professionals from multiple departments.
- Deflected 50% increase in electricity costs by designing/installing power factor correction systems.
- Reduced water usage by 80% by developing new cooling water temperature control system.
- Led national expansion of single-serve potato chip product—building U.S. volume +33%—by utilizing U.S. volume projections, international test market demands, and available capacity.
- Increased revenue by recruiting, training, and organizing efficient contract staff capable of faster processing time that optimized sales representatives' performance.

- Began employment as fax runner whose superiors recognized exemplary professional skills and unsurpassed work ethic; promoted to administrative assistant, and promoted again to senior administrative assistant within a year.
- Achieved 36% rating increase in customer survey scores by creating and implementing two new staff training programs that heightened levels of guest satisfaction.
- Increased sales revenue by $15 million in one year by assembling dynamic marketing team, coaching team members, and implementing highly effective marketing strategy.
- Reduced unnecessary book purchases by developing Excel spreadsheet book inventory.
- Raised $250K in one evening by coordinating 85 volunteers for school auction/dinner and through sales of 800 silent and 40 live-auction items.
- Facilitated 55% increase in customer satisfaction and 50% increase in employee job satisfaction by flattening hierarchy from 10 functional areas to just two, guiding employees to redefine their jobs, creating efficient work processes, eliminating redundancies, and eradicating paperwork in organization formerly unresponsive to clients as well as inefficient, bureaucratic, and apathetic.
- Boosted sales rate by 200% in first year and 400% over five years, successfully capturing majority of engineering specification market.
- Revived branch image, upgraded technology and equipment, and reestablished company as industry leader by increasing sales dramatically.
- Achieved 95% spend capture, 35% system operating and maintenance cost reduction, increased order visibility and leverage position, and enhanced supplier relationship management by executing successful integration of business units' procurement and payables systems and processes.
- Reduced annual consulting costs by $1.4M, streamlined development processes, facilitated rapid turnaround of customer requests, and enhanced internal application-development and application-support capabilities by developing and executing plan to in-source numerous key IT functions.
- Achieved 25% call-back rate, 30% sales increase, and a reopened revenue stream by executing direct-mail initiative to contact dormant customers to provide name recognition reminder and publish service-option details.
- Saved company $13.75 million—$1.75 million in first year and $4 million annually for three consecutive years—by conceiving, designing, and strategizing to bring branch computer maintenance in-house.

(continued)

(continued)

- Saved weeks in project time by instituting structured project-management methodology.
- Increased recoveries from less than 2% of paid to 5.7% of paid, resulting in $39.6 million in increased recoverables, by creating "Third-Party Recovery Recognition Templates."
- Reduced customer requests from 500 to 12 within three months by designing and implementing centralized customer task-tracking system.
- Reduced errors, saved time, achieved nearly a 100% paperless environment, and saved money by implementing central Web-based database that houses all client data, realizing remarkable return on equipment investment in less than a year.

Creating a Resume Addendum to Enhance Your Resume's Storytelling

Even if you've used storytelling to describe your accomplishments in your resume, space limitations have likely prevented you from providing much detail. Deborah Wile Dib, a CEO coach with multiple certifications in resume writing and career coaching, is an enthusiastic champion of the concept of resume addenda. Noting that these story-based addenda are "a good read," she variously titles them "Critical Leadership Initiatives," "Marketing Milestones," "Performance Milestones," "Key Engagements" (for a consultant), "Career Success and Distinctions," and "Major Campaigns." Dib encourages clients to identify their "career-defining accomplishments" and then rank-order the top five that align best with the job seeker's targeted employers.

For Dib, most accomplishments can be summed up in the phrase "accomplished solutions provider." The employer, Dib notes, is primarily interested in whether the candidate can solve problems and make/save money. The addendum supplies information—that the more concise resume can't accomplish—about the challenge the candidate faced and the process used to achieve the result, Dib says. To enhance the storytelling power of her resumes and addenda, Dib sometimes even breaks the cardinal resume rule against using the pronoun "I" in her documents.

Also touting the idea of the resume addendum is well-known resume writer and career author Louise Kursmark, who refers to these addenda as "ROI documents," replete with stories that illustrate the Return on Investment the employer will gain in hiring the candidate. Kursmark's own special twist on the resume addendum is the Job Proposal, which tells a future story of what the candidate can do for the employer. The proposal presents the candidate's understanding of the employer's challenge, includes a section titled "My Value" that explains how the candidate is the most qualified person to meet the challenge, and offers a "Proposed Solution."

Dib cautions that not everyone involved in the hiring process likes resume addenda, and my Ph.D. research bears out that caution. But as long as the employer also has your "story lite" resume, he or she can choose whether or not to review the addendum. Some recruiters in the focus-group research liked the option of being able to obtain additional information from addenda. One participant said, "I like addenda because they don't get in my way, but if I choose to delve deeper when presenting to a hiring manager, the info is there."

The addendum can also make an excellent artifact for your career portfolio. (See chapter 6 for more on portfolios.)

Are Resumes Dying?

With some career experts predicting that traditional resumes may be on their way out, readers may question the notion of the storytelling resume. Citing online recruiting expert John Sullivan as well as Allan Schweyer of the Human Capital Institute, Dib prognosticates that "within a few years most companies who are hiring or recruiting online will use e-profiles in place of the traditional resume. E-profiles allow access to information that is sorted and easy to use." Dib's finger is on the pulse of those who predict that paperless recruiting will become the norm.

While the resume may disappear from the online job search and morph into new forms and spinoffs, it will still be used for mailing, networking, and interviewing. No matter what form the resume takes, expert wordsmithing will still be required, Dib notes, "to compose keyword-rich online profiles in resume builders, and to develop compelling success stories for interviews." A focus-group participant agrees, stating that "in the business world, there will always be a time and place when candidates will need a quick, concise, easily accessible summary of their skills. I think technology will continue to streamline the job application process, and resumes will adapt accordingly but never go away completely."

It's also just possible that the current business trend toward storytelling will move the resume to a more rather than less narrative form. As businesspeople recognize the power of storytelling and eschew emotionless data, PowerPoint presentations, dry analytical facts, and terse bullet points, they will be drawn to story-based resumes. As *A Whole New Mind* author Daniel Pink warns, "minimizing the importance of story places you in professional and personal peril."

Employers and recruiters express a constant concern about finding candidates who are a good fit with their organizations, who will perform, and who will get results. Given that they fret about the ability to predict candidate performance before hiring, they should welcome information in the resume that helps them to get to know more about the candidate rather than less. In fact, it is not decision-makers' distaste for rich information that is driving the current trend toward standardized profile forms that enable employers to compare apples to apples; instead, it is the revolution in Internet recruiting and job hunting that has inundated employers with too many resumes to deal with. But as Pink points out, we have a "hunger for what stories can provide—context enriched by emotion, a deeper understanding of how we fit in and why that matters."

Sample Story-Based Resumes and Addenda

The following section contains the following story-based resumes and addenda to give you a better idea how to use storytelling in these documents:

- Walter Dietz Story Resume
- Sean Patrick Story Resume Addendum: Leadership Profile
- Wesley Edwards Story Resume
- Zhang Li "Story-Lite" Resume followed by Executive Performance Highlights Addendum
- Paul Goldfarb Story Resume Addendum: Leadership Initiatives Summary
- Mathias Carroll Projects Supplement
- Georgia Lutz Bio Addendum

WALTER DIETZ

123 Westfield Avenue ▪ Ash Ferry, NY 10522 ▪ 212.123.4567 ▪ wdietz125@aol.net

SENIOR HUMAN RESOURCES MANAGER

ORGANIZATIONAL CULTURE AND VISION ▪ PROACTIVE BUSINESS LEADERSHIP

POLICY ▪ PROCESS ▪ SYSTEMS

BUILDING OUTSTANDING WORKPLACES AND PERFORMANCE-DRIVEN ORGANIZATIONS

Strategic business partner and catalyst for innovative initiatives that address today's business challenges of attaining revenue goals, controlling expenses, satisfying customers, and attracting/retaining talent while achieving business and profitability objectives. Capable of transitioning underperforming organizations into highly effective ones as well as leading organizations through accelerated growth or rapid change.

KEY ACCOMPLISHMENTS

- Built high-performing, results-driven staffing function in a highly competitive, rapid-growth sales environment.
- Devised a comprehensive succession-planning and leadership-development program.
- Resolved complex, sensitive bicultural staff-relations issues following merger.
- Coached executive management team on planning and communications skills to increase productivity levels.

KNOWLEDGE AND EXPERTISE

- Strategic Planning/Implementation
- Restructuring and Revitalization
- Employee Relations
- Succession Planning
- Training/Employee Development
- Leadership Development
- Recruitment and Staffing
- HRIS Technology
- Climate Surveys
- Selection Techniques/Assessment Tools
- Organizational Development/Change
- EEO/Regulatory Compliance
- Benefits/Compensation Management

PROFESSIONAL EXPERIENCE

Regional Director, MET, Inc., New York, New York **2005–Present**

Subsidiary of Cendant Corporation and the largest residential real-estate brokerage company in the country.

Senior HR Executive for 3 MET divisions, Habitats (rentals), The Alliance Group (re-sales), and The HomeLife Group (new development). Hold complete strategic planning, leadership, and operating management responsibility for all HR activities. Lead a direct staff of 8 HR professionals.

- Restructured the HR department, consolidating 3 separate departments into 1. Reduced costs by sharing applicant databases and leveraging recruiting activities for multiple positions. Increased employee retention and satisfaction by providing more opportunities for advancement.
- Strengthened relationships with functional departments, making HR a strategic partner in process development, staffing, and employee relations.
- Collaborated with senior staff to manage the post-merger integration of two new development companies. Streamlined and redefined workflow, roles and responsibilities, and compensation/pay practices. Restored employee confidence and trust, overcoming initial resistance to change as employees moved from a privately held company to a publicly traded corporation. Persuaded key contributors to stay with the organization.
- Simplified sales employment process and agreements, eliminating time-consuming contract negotiations to quickly fill critical sales positions. Modified the sales compensation plan, implementing a pay-for-performance model using incentives and bonuses to motivate performance while reducing base pay salaries.

Figure 4.1: Walter Dietz Story Resume. This fictionalized resume was prepared by Roberta Gamza, Career Ink, phone/fax (303) 955-3065, toll-free (877) 581-6063, www.careerink.com and is reprinted with permission.

WALTER DIETZ

Page 2

HR Consultant/Executive Coach, At Your Best Coaching, Ash Ferry, NY 2004–2005

Recruited by the president of an energy services company to effect behavior changes in the management team resulting in increased performance/productivity and to provide staffing and employee-relations leadership.

- Coached staff members individually, helping them to identify and overcome barriers to their success.
- Devised and established HR policies and procedures.
- Advised managers on employee-relations matters as well as staffing and candidate selection.

Vice President, Human Resources, Action Technologies, White Plains, NY 2000–2004

Promoted from Regional HR Manager to lead the corporate HR function during rapid growth through acquisition and expansion in the Northeast region. Participated in positioning the company for sale in 2004.

- Realigned/restructured the sales organization to support the new business objectives and strategy. Recruited and hired a new Sales EVP. Defined sales roles and created new position profiles.
- Shortened hiring cycle to meet the demands of accelerated growth. Selected and implemented an assessment tool to evaluate both new candidates and current employees.
- Reduced costs while maintaining comparable benefits by outsourcing payroll and benefits. Served as champion of the new provider and program to preserve employee confidence.
- Elevated employee morale and increased confidence through communication forums, employee opinion survey, and incentive bonuses in lieu of merit increases during the "dotcom bust." Created an environment of inclusion, open communication, and honesty during times of change.

Assistant Vice President, Bank of Tokyo, New York, NY 1997–2000

Challenged to lead integration efforts following the merger of 2 banks with vastly different cultures and management styles. Reestablished balance in the workforce and addressed staff-relations issues that arose post merger. Advised/trained expatriate management staff in EEO law, coaching and counseling, and performance management.

- Employed the Birkman Method team-building instrument to foster open communications, build trust, and create a much-needed unified culture among the Tokyo Mitsubishi Securities group.
- Resolved employee-relations issues that emerged in the post-merger environment. Earned the confidence and trust of the expatriate managers, helping them to transform and strengthen relationships with the existing staff.
- Designed and deployed a job-specific and goal-based Performance Management program. Trained and advised management staff on how to apply the new program.

Human Resources Manager, Xerox Business Solutions, New York, NY 1990–1997

Began tenure as the first recruiter hired. Promoted to HR Manager supporting 1,000 employees in 9 locations.

- Implemented annual climate survey that became an integral part of the company culture. Survey feedback resulted in actionable plans that contributed to the overall growth and success of the company.
- Created a highly effective/responsive staffing function during rapid growth; devised a comprehensive leadership-development program and succession plan.
- Reengineered and integrated back-office functions to create a single, highly efficient order-fulfillment customer interface. Cross-trained employees on multiple functions to facilitate a single point for problem resolution.

EDUCATION / PROFESSIONAL CERTIFICATIONS / AFFILIATIONS

B.A. English, State University of New York, Stony Brook, NY
Intensive Executive Development Workshop, Farr Associates
Certified Strategic Corporate Coach, Corporate Coach U
Certified Targeted Selection Administrator, Developmental Dimensions International (DDI)
Member, Society for Human Resource Management (SHRM) and International Coach Federation (ICF)

Leadership Profile

SEAN PATRICK, FMA, RPA

LEADERSHIP SUCCESSES AS DIRECTOR OF ENGINEERING
HILTON HOTEL, STANFORD, CT

DEPARTMENT OPERATIONS & FINANCE MANAGEMENT

"Sean is able to keep the team's efforts focused on the most productive activities. He is a total hotel team player. He has positioned the engineering department to be extremely supportive of all operations and focused on internal and external customers as the priority."
—*William Hagendorf, General Manager*

Challenge: Position facilities engineering function / department as a P&L partner.

Action: Created virtually "self-managed" department—implemented monthly and quarterly budget tracking / financial analysis system, streamlined business processes, and delegated administrative functions.

Result: Contributed as much as $88,136 to company's bottom line in 2001 and succeeded in operating the engineering department at or below budget every year (despite facility's 25+ years age).

Analysis: With my team handling many of the daily administrative and financial functions, I could focus on achieving new goals in project management, customer service, and relationship building in support of the brand.

PROJECT & BRAND MANAGEMENT

"Sean promotes an atmosphere where individuals can be creative. He rewards independent thinking and reasonable risk taking, and supports people even if a new approach is unsuccessful."
—*William Hagendorf, General Manager*

Challenge: Manage renovation—combining historical style with the Hilton Hotel brand—of 1905 Normandy-style estate of Charles T. Rothbert.

Action: Conveyed the Hilton Hotel & Resorts brand and style to architects and interior designers. Provided creative and managerial oversight throughout complete reconceptualization and reconstruction of the property. Selected color schemes, wall covering, flooring, carpet, lighting, signage, and artwork.

Result: Completion of this $700,000 project drove 34% revenue increase from renovated property's corporate meetings and private events. Met all municipal code standards while maintaining historical feel.

Analysis: This project showcased the core of my value—outstanding technical qualifications and extensive experience managing large-scale, complex projects; combined with creativity, style, and unwavering consciousness of the importance of the corporate message and brand.

FACILITIES & BUSINESS MANAGEMENT

"Sean is a champion of change and takes a positive and open-minded approach to new initiatives…very good at looking at all aspects of a new process or initiative to make sure all possible outcomes are considered."
—*William Hagendorf, General Manager*

Challenge: Contribute in a key way to corporate-mandated business initiatives and regulatory compliance matters involving facilities management. Prove my value in the role of Director of Engineering.

Action: Developed and executed plan for reducing use and emissions of refrigerants to lowest possible levels, and maximizing proficiency of recapture and recycling. Trained five HVAC mechanics and other technical services personnel in new service and repair procedures.

Result: Brought property into compliance with 1990 amendments to Title VI Stratospheric Ozone Protection Section 608 of the Clean Air Act as outlined in National Recycling and Emissions Reduction Program. Earned "Environmental Leadership Award" by the Environmental Advisory Committee of Stamford, CT, on Earth Day 1998. Earned executive committee's endorsement for promotion to Director of Engineering.

198-27 37th Ave., Flushing, NY 11358 • Home: 718-555-5555 • Cell: 718-000-0000 • Fax: 718-111-1111
E-mail: SeanPatrick65@msn.com • E-mail: SPatrick@nextel.blackberry.net

Figure 4.2: Sean Patrick Story Resume Addendum: Leadership Profile. This fictionalized resume addendum was prepared by Deb Dib, Advantage Resumes of NY, Executive Power Coach, Executive Power Marketing, Executive Power Brand, (631) 475-8513, fax (501) 421-7790, e-mail debdib@executivepowergroup.com, www.executivepowergroup.com, and is reprinted with permission.

SEAN PATRICK, FMA, RPA **PAGE 2 OF 2**

FACILITIES & BUSINESS MANAGEMENT, continued

Analysis: Professional credentials (certified by the Refrigeration Service Engineers Society), technical proficiency, and a personal commitment to making a difference—contributed to the growth, profitability, brand, and competitive positioning of the company.

COST REDUCTION & ROI IMPROVEMENT

"Conscientious about implementing organizational changes and always accepts such challenges graciously—made contributions in communicating benefits of changes and getting necessary resources."
—Marta Zinn, General Manager

Challenge: Reduce facility's total energy consumption.

Action: Led development and deployment—in conjunction with Energy Conservation Committee—of a strategic property energy plan that outlined/prioritized short- and long-term initiatives and objectives. Benchmarked efforts and results with Energy Star to ensure optimal success of strategies and initiatives.

Result: Delivered 7% reduction in utilities consumption in 2008—against 5% target. On track to achieve 2% consumption reduction in 2009.

Strength: I am an initiator and facilitator of performance improvement, cost containment, energy conservation, and culture change. I use innovation, resourcefulness, and tenacity to deliver exceptional, not expected, results.

FAST-TRACK PROJECT MANAGEMENT

"Sean's dealings and communications with diverse groups are outstanding."
—William Hagendorf, General Manager

Challenge: Complete major exterior renovation project—replace outdoor pool's entire wooden deck with 4,225-sq.-ft. Unilock paver patio/perimeter landscaping in time for critical Memorial Day business and events.

Action: Managed fast-track project lifecycle—approved architectural design, acquired permits, negotiated with vendor, administered/controlled budget, and supervised site activities.

Result: New patio was credited with contributing to 25% increase in membership revenues in 2003. Brought project in on time and within budget.

Analysis: No project is too challenging. Over the course of my 15-year career, I have encountered and overcome virtually every possible challenge, obstacle, and constraint, and have always prevailed.

EMERGENCY PLANNING & RESPONSE

"Sean explores the processes that cause events rather than thinking solely about the event."
—Marta Zinn, General Manager

Challenge: Mitigate operational risk and ensure the safety of the property's guests and staff.

Action: Trained management staff and other stakeholders in principles of Comprehensive Emergency Management (CEM), developed action plans, formulated policies, and led monthly business-continuity meetings.

Result: Provided property with a best-in-class emergency response and business-continuity plan. The effectiveness of the plan was demonstrated during the "2008 blackout," when our property was the only Hilton hotel that realized a profit on that night. Guests were calmly and orderly escorted to the well-lit pool deck for beverages and songs while the facilities and security teams completed a series of checks and controls.

Analysis: I take my responsibilities (including the safety of others) seriously and I have acquired and maintained comprehensive knowledge of contemporary business continuity, security, and emergency-response/disaster-recovery principles.

Wesley Edwards

24152 Santa Teresa Avenue, Mission Viejo, CA 92692
Phone: 949-555-5555, Cell Phone: 702-555-5555, E-mail: Wes702@yahoo.com

CUSTOMER SERVICE ~ ORGANIZATION ~ COMMUNICATION ~ LEADERSHIP

Customer Relations Director

Translating organizational goals into precisely crafted customer and human-relations practices through innovative process improvement and multidimensional communication strategies.

Professional Profile

- Accomplished 5-Star–certified customer-development professional with significant success record in auto dealership customer relations achieved through process organization and improvement, executing training programs, establishing high performance standards, and strengthening supportive administrative practices.
- Strong communicator with exceptional organizational skills and ability to manage multiple situations and projects simultaneously with focus, direction, and enthusiasm.
- Motivated achiever who uses problem-solving skills to synthesize and apply information quickly while adapting to new situations seamlessly to make an immediate contribution.
- Human-relations pro who excels in team-building and leadership roles, managing, training, and directing multidepartmental staff initiatives, as well as developing, coordinating, organizing, and executing public-relations campaigns and large-group events.

Professional Experience

Customer Relations Director and 5-Star Coordinator, *DodgeLand USA—Dodge Automotive Dealer,* Las Vegas, NV, 2006 to 2009

- Transformed dealership's failing reputation from prior ownership into thriving automotive sales and service entity by implementing 5-Star evaluative and strategic methodology.
- Achieved 5-Star Dealer Certification through increased sales satisfaction score, customer-service satisfaction ratings, and vehicles fixed during first visit into dealer service department.
- More than doubled Customer Satisfaction Index (CSI) scores from 40% to 88% in four months by initiating phone campaign to proactively resolve issues.
- Ensured customer satisfaction by conducting 100% customer follow-up on sales and service, completing detailed trend analysis, addressing customer issues, and reviewing customer feedback in management meetings.
- Played instrumental role in igniting dramatic growth in sales and customer satisfaction for dealership by establishing and managing Business Development Center (BDC) from ground up.
- Attained virtually paperless environment by streamlining processes and improving efficiency.
- Propelled dealership into top third of Dodge dealers nationwide by implementing personnel training to reach certified BDC status in just four months, compared to one-year norm.
- Broadened dealership exposure by overseeing creation and maintenance of dealership Web site as well as establishing a presence on corporate site, showing strong, steady increase in site traffic.
- Tracked $450,000 in rebate/incentive capital each month and recovered lost revenue by resolving data errors and maintaining contact with corporate offices/customers to settle outstanding debts.
- Ensured repeat business by performing all new and certified vehicle deliveries and boosted customer satisfaction throughout revitalized sales process.

Figure 4.3: Wesley Edwards Story Resume, written by Katharine Hansen.

Sales Associate/General Motors Buypower Manager, *Pontiac-Cadillac of Sioux Falls,* Sioux Falls, SD, 2003 to 2006

- Generated increasing volume of walk-in and Internet-driven automobile sales for sister store by actively cultivating leads, referrals, and sales opportunities.
- Surpassed company quota of nine car sales monthly throughout tenure by selling an average of 15 vehicles, and as many as 20 in one month, while maintaining extraordinary 90% CSI rating.
- Excelled as top performer and leader among sales consultants through mentoring sales associates.
- Played key role in dealership's dramatic rise in ranking for Pontiac car sales, from 32nd to 2nd in zone, top 100 in the U.S., and 6th in zone for all GM lines, including trucks, by responding effectively to customer inquiries with information and incentives to visit dealership.
- Achieved GM Certification as Sales Consultant, Finance and Insurance Manager, Used Car Sales Manager, and New Car Sales Manager by completing intensive training in all major sales-related areas.

Manager, *Enterprise Rent-A-Car,* San Antonio, TX, 2000 to 2003

- Rose quickly through several management levels—trainee to the third level of management in just seven months—within nation's largest car-rental company, culminating in playing key role on team that managed customer-service lot and shuttle operations for San Antonio Airport branch.
- Satisfied customers by providing them with prompt, efficient service and regularly oversaw vehicle returns, cleaning, fueling, and placement of 500-car fleet.
- Earned two Marketing Excellence awards and two White Shirt awards through generating new business and performing acts of excellence in customer service acknowledged by specific customers.
- Streamlined shuttle rotation and customer flow by instituting shuttle-fleet management system.
- Halted loss of fuel cards at a cost of $80 each by initiating employee accountability system.

AREAS OF EXPERTISE

→ Customer Development
→ Human Relations
→ Research and Planning
→ Interdepartmental Liaison
→ Elevate Standards of Service
→ Process Improvement
→ Internal/External Customer Service
→ Communication
→ Public Relations and Event Planning
→ Administration and Management
→ Administrative Decision-Making
→ Hiring and Workforce Supervision
→ Revenue Recovery
→ Problem-Solving
→ Training/Coaching/Mentoring
→ Problem Identification/Resolution
→ Scheduling/Planning/Organization
→ Sales and Marketing

CERTIFICATIONS AND PROFESSIONAL DEVELOPMENT

Certifications:

5-Star Coordinator, Las Vegas, NV, 2008, 2009
Sales Manager Certification, Las Vegas, NV, 2007, 2008
Certificate in Supervisory Skills, Las Vegas, NV, 2007

ZHANG LE

INTERNATIONAL SENIOR EXECUTIVE
U.S.-ASIAN MARKETS • START-UPS and TURNAROUNDS • BUSINESS DEVELOPMENT

PROFILE

- High-profile senior executive extensively experienced in delivering bold marketing, communications, and business-development programs for U.S. and Asian interests.
- Savvy marketer who initiates and develops profitable B2B relationships for leading clients in the region.
- Profit-minded professional who drives aggressive revenue growth and market entry/expansion by using talent for connecting mission, product, and service to untapped niches.
- Exceptional communicator who brings multicultural and trilingual (Mandarin-Cantonese-English) advantages in leveraging relationships with senior corporate and public leaders.
- Skilled negotiator who gains the edge in hammering out agreements by navigating diverse cultural environments.
- Motivated achiever who earned Excellence in Marketing Award and recognition by the Chinese government and private industry for outstanding contributions to promoting Chinese tourism worldwide.

PROFESSIONAL HISTORY

Principal/Senior Consultant, ZLE INTERNATIONAL CONSULTANTS, New York, NY, 1996 to Present

- Own and operate management consulting practice representing key Asian and U.S.-based corporations in processed product energy, broadcast, advertising, PR, finance, tourism, and Internet industries.
- Provide strategic planning, international business development, marketing, corporate communications, sales, and general-management services to companies globally.
- Plan and manage complete engagement cycle—from initial contact with C-level executives, project proposals, fee structuring, and negotiations, to service and product deliveries.

Managing Director, INTERNATIONAL ACE, New York, NY, 1993 to 1996

- Managed market entry of international barter and trading company currently generating more than US$700M in annual revenues.
- Oversaw full executive functions, including strategic planning, operations, finance, P&L, marketing, HR, and administration.

Managing Director, International Marketing. CHINESE MINISTRY OF TOURISM, Beijing, China, and New York, NY, 1990 to 1993

- Promoted from senior regional management position to international marketing role, overseeing business planning, operations, and communications efforts.
- Directed operations for ministry's 15 locations worldwide, representing US$6.5B in annual revenues.
- Oversaw $45M marketing budget and managed 150-member multicultural team.
- Created and led specialized programs to advance China's third-largest industry, international tourism.

EDUCATION

- Bachelor of Science in Marketing, Columbia University, New York, NY
- Continuing Education: Seminars on management, strategic marketing, and international business at universities and private institutes in the U.S. and China

Figure 4.4: Zhang Le Story-Lite Resume, written by Katharine Hansen.

Paul Goldfarb — **Leadership Initiatives Summary**

Senior Global Operations Management Executive — **404.555.1922**
Delivering impossible advances in key operational imperatives — pgoldfarb@emailme.net

"Paul came into our organization at a time of extreme growth. He was able to streamline our operations and increase our efficiencies and client service levels tenfold. We tripled our assets and were able to focus on continuing to obtain new business vs. sales folks trying to run operations. I always found Paul to be extremely professional, loyal, and dedicated. Paul Goldfarb makes things happen!"

—Heather Reston, Marketing Manager, Worldwide Investment Services, Inc.

Entrepreneurial Startups, Marketing Programs, and Sustainable Growth

Chief Executive Officer—Summit Business Strategies

Designed robust marketing programs to move two entrepreneurial ventures from vision to startup and profitable business.

Client 1—in second year of startup

- Crafted a multifocused marketing approach zeroing in on specific demographics of total market potential, directly reaching 6 demographic consumer segments.
- Grew sales month over month by 30% to make first-year sales goal within 10 months.
- Propelled client to hit third-year goals in year two.
- Expanded markets to reach over 400,000 potential customers within one week, outdistancing previous rate of only 45,000 prospects per month.

Client 2—in third month of startup

- Refined original product concept and gained highly favorable consumer response. Directed product development by tracking consumer and market focus research.
- Marketed product to 4 key large distribution business partners, outsourcing fulfillment to one source that will service all 4.
- Saved $5,000 per month redirecting physical office and warehouse.

Crisis and Turnaround Management

President—Pinnacle Investment Services, Worldwide Investment, Inc.

Situation & Challenges

In 1997, Worldwide Investment Services merged directly into Pinnacle while Pinnacle faced the impending retirement of the existing president, along with a split into two poorly functioning operating centers. The new second entity was led by an ineffectual manager who lacked vision and direction.

The atmosphere was one of overall divisiveness, animosity, and backstabbing. Only minimal service and processing requirements were met despite climbing backlogs in processing; division turnover was at 25%; growth was uncontrolled; and risk, which was at a dangerous level, was being ignored.

Actions

- ➢ **Turned around several failing components within division (client service, performance quality, metric guidelines) to develop a truly synergistic organization.**
- ➢ **Introduced Change Management to all managers from supervisor and up and brought consistency to every process.** Created a new wholistic vision, segregated into understandable, achievable bites, to handle challenges each stakeholder faced.

Figure 4.5: Paul Goldfarb Story Resume Addendum: Leadership Initiatives Summary. This fictionalized resume addendum was prepared by Meg Guiseppi of Executive Resume Branding (division of Resumes Plus LLC), (973) 726-0757, fax (973) 726-0121, e-mail meg@ExecutiveResumeBranding.com, www.ExecutiveResumeBranding.com, and is reprinted with permission.

Paul Goldfarb **Leadership Initiatives Summary / Page 2**

Actions, continued

- **Stopped excessive and extremely expensive staff turnover:**
  - Launched incentives and created professional/business career opportunities, while supporting quality associates content to perform optimally at the same level in the same department.
  - Staggered shifts to align with flow of daily processing and allowed for flexible scheduling.
  - Improved communications and cooperation among senior management/leadership.
  - Reevaluated and shifted new-hire requirements. Moved away from degree-only candidates toward highly qualified nondegreed people and set in place a true professional track for advancement.
- **United independent, self-serving group of 7 senior vice presidents intent on protecting their own territories:**
  - Deepened their commitment toward unified leadership from the top down to advance opportunities, rewards, recognition, and success.
  - Clearly communicated expectation to them and introduced annual goals/measurements and long-range strategic planning for budgeting, vision execution, and personal improvement.

Impact & Analysis

- Reduced turnover 50% and blended 5 operating entities into one.
- Led, inspired, and built a cohesive, knowledgeable team completely satisfied with their jobs and ignited to excel. Empowered them to know their customers and how to deliver quality experiences to them.
- Reduced costs through more efficient workforce, increased employee metrics and service quality, and gained respect organization-wide for the team.
- Achieved a collaborative, creative environment supporting change and exceeding customers' needs and expectations.

MATHIAS CARROLL

91110 Forest Dr., Apt 126, Houston, TX 77096 ◆ Phone: 713-555-5555 ◆ E-mail: carroll_m@hotmail.com

PROJECT HIGHLIGHTS

Projects/ Deliverables	Challenge	Action and Results
As Product Manager, Norwich Community Bank		
Tax Payments and Data Import Enhancements on Internet	Tax payment and import functionality on the Automated Clearing House (ACH) module of Internet.	Oversaw product delivery and all marketing. Achieved successful, first-in-market implementation.
Conversion of Clients to New Internet System	Changes to Internet system warranted customer system changes.	Successful implementation with minimal customer issues.
Transmission System Enhancements	Antiquated transmission hardware system; $2+ million capital request had been consistently denied in previous years.	Successfully collaborated with team to bridge past failings and placed product spin on a business case, which was approved.
Enhancements to External Communication to Clients	Customer correspondence was inconsistent with established brand image and noncompliance risk existed.	First to visualize and implement new use for established internal customer setup system. Designed/implemented automated customer letter trigger to ensure consistent brand image and that important correspondence is sent to client while contributing to operational efficiency; became the standard for all departmental products.
Automated Pay/Draw Mechanism via Internet	Product enhancement needed for Business Credit Line customers to initiate requests via Internet.	Developed system specifications for product; first to establish cross-functional teams needed to implement properly and effectively.
Tax Payment Option on VRU Menu	Tax Payment via telephone was not part of long-established and marketed 800 number.	Oversaw idea and implementation, resulting in crossing business segments, which in turn reduced another customer channel and increased exposure of product to customers and sales.
Next-Generation Internet Product	Vendor selection of next-generation Internet solution.	Played key role on core team that oversaw acquisition of a new vendor, which exceeded $2 million purchase.
ACH Risk Initiative	Risk initiative designed to automate funding of ACH files and broaden credit policies to enable more customer penetration while managing risk.	First in market. Developed strategies to address gap in training and simplify a complicated process. Exceeded expectations and goals of project, garnering executive leadership praise on implementation success. Market studies showed lead in positioning and also exposed larger customer segment to product traditionally targeted for large corporate clients.

Figure 4.6: Mathias Carroll Project Highlights Resume Addendum, written by Katharine Hansen.

Career Biography

GEORGIA LUTZ

Senior Scientist/Country Liaison Officer/AGRINET Coordinator
International Agriculture Improvement Center

I am a management and agriculture professional with more than 14 years of research, capacity building, and supervisory experience in international agriculture. I currently execute my mission to empower national research institutions to meet the needs of smallholder farmers by excelling in multiple functions at the International Agriculture Improvement Center, based in the Philippines. These functions include senior scientist and the center's country liaison officer for the Philippines, managing the center and representing it in the host country. Since 1998, I have also engaged in extensive networking and outreach as coordinator of the Agricultural Biotechnology Network (AGRINET), overseeing administration of a training, research, and information network involving the Center and nine national research institutes/universities in six Asian countries.

Currently, I also serve as interim coordinator of a new applied center project in Asia linking science with farmers, using participatory approaches that involve many stakeholders in the community. The Asian Development Bank funded this project based on a grant proposal that I wrote with input from center colleagues.

In my multiple roles, I contribute to project planning and budgeting, as well as guide the implementation of network and country work plans, analyzing problems that prevent achieving those plans, ensuring accountability, monitoring results, and proposing solutions to keep projects on track, on time, and on budget.

As a vital component in building an enabling environment for scientists in national programs, I collaborate in bringing visibility to and encouraging national support for the AGRINET project by interacting effectively with senior-level government and university officials (including members of the AGRINET Steering Committee), donors, and various stakeholders. Through my leadership, AGRINET now enjoys a reputation as a credible, active network for crop improvement in Asia, as documented in an impact-assessment study of the network, which is available upon request.

Previously, I served as a long-term consultant at the International Agriculture Research Institute, overseeing technology development/transfer in the Agriculture Biotechnology Network. I adapted molecular marker applications to developing-country conditions and supported their integration into rice breeding programs.

Productive interactions with various stakeholders in a culturally sensitive manner have been a hallmark of my positions in the center, and my success has been measured in the "collaborative advantage" that I created through these interdisciplinary, multistakeholder, and multicountry partnerships. I possess first-hand knowledge and understanding of the workings of international agricultural research centers, the environment in which they operate, and their interactions with donors and various stakeholders. My strengths are my on-the-ground experience in partnership building, along with effective interpersonal and negotiation skills.

My research in the use of biotechnologies as research tools has spanned a variety of areas, including plant-microbe interactions, as well as rice and maize molecular genetics. As a scientist at the center, my experience has continued to expand, and I have enhanced my skills set, from project management to increasingly responsible leadership roles. During the recent center strategic-planning exercise, I played a key role on the Task Force on Partners/Networks/Systems.

I earned my Ph.D. and MS in microbiology from the University of Hawaii and also hold a master's degree in public administration (MPA) and a bachelor's degree in biology from the University of the Philippines. I continue my professional growth through numerous leadership and management courses.

Figure 4.7: Georgia Lutz Career Biography, written by Katharine Hansen.

Summary

In an era in which resumes have become increasingly standardized, you have an opportunity to stand out by telling compelling stories in subtle ways in your resume. From conveying the story of yourself in a Qualifications Summary or Professional Profile section atop your resume, to bullet points that tell the story of your accomplishments, you can draw the reader into your job history. Supplemental documents enable you to expand on your success stories.

CHAPTER 5

Cover Letters That Tell a Story

Unlike resumes with their clipped bullet points, cover letters offer you much wider latitude to tell stories because letters are quite compatible with the narrative form. You can engage the employer, make an emotional connection, show results, and become instantly memorable by writing at least one paragraph in the form of a powerful story. Not all employers read cover letters (about a third don't), but those who read them do truly read the letter, unlike the resume, which they almost always skim.

In this chapter I'll give you some ideas of the types of stories you can tell in your cover letter for maximum impact. Then I'll reveal some of the do's and don'ts for storytelling cover letters. All of this is followed by some excellent examples of letters that tell stories.

Types of Stories You Can Tell in a Cover Letter

Cover letters provide opportunities that resumes don't to inject your personality. They enable the reader to see where you're coming from and how well you fit the targeted job. Stories offer a meaningful and compelling way to frame the type of information that helps build a connection between you and the reader. You can use a wide range of stories in your cover letters—from describing early interest or passion for a career field to detailing successful projects, accomplishments, solutions, results, and more.

Stories of Early Career Interest and Determination

You can tell stories about how you first became interested in your career goal and how determined you were to achieve it. A participant in cover-letter focus-group research conducted for this book said that the following example "creates a vivid picture in your mind and leaves a memorable impression with the reader."

One of my most profound memories as a young child was the day I first flew on an airplane. I was traveling with my family to California, and I still remember the feeling of excitement as I held my mother's hand and climbed the stairs into the immense red, white, and blue plane. That was my first of many flights on Delta, and I have never forgotten it. I am interested in fostering that same excitement in others by working for Delta as a training instructor.

More samples of early career interest:

Six years ago when you hired me for my first job, I wonder if you realized that the experience would inspire my career. I want to thank you for giving me that first opportunity to explore retail, not only because I enjoy the work so much, but because I've learned enough to know that I want to make a long-term commitment to this field.

You would have to look far and wide to find someone who could bring as much enthusiasm and creativity as I can to the position of assistant creative director of StoryDance. Ever since I attended StoryDance's performances as a young child, I've had a vision of the kind of creativity and energy I could add to the program. I carried that vision all the way to college, where I majored in theater and minored in dance.

Stories of Motivation, Enthusiasm, and Passion

Words such as "passion" and "excited" jumped out at a focus-group participant when evaluating the sample letter shown on page 100. "These are things an employer looks for in a candidate," the participant said. "You don't want to hire someone who is simply there to do a job. You want them to have a desire and motivation not only for the position, but to help the company grow as well—and using those words depicts just that." More examples:

While completing my degree in media communications and technology last year, I cultivated a true passion for video work that I would like to contribute to Southeast News Video.

Every morning I kick off the sheets and leap out of bed—thrilled to greet my new day and eager to engage all the challenges I will encounter. I can imagine the many challenges you face as the market leader that could benefit from my performance-management expertise as your Product Support and Training Manager.

Stories About Projects and Results

You can also tell stories describing specific projects you've led or collaborated on, including results. Here are two examples:

> *More than five years of high performance in retail banking and the direct-investment industry in a recently emerging market—Vietnam—has provided me with exceptional experiences and strong connections with decision-making officials in the private and public sectors. Leading a small team to reorganize a Vietnamese bank virtually from scratch, I was apprehensive about the overwhelming challenges, yet excited to exercise my leadership skills. The result exceeded all expectations; not only did we stabilize the bank, but we also managed to raise $2M in equity. After completing the successful reorganization, I earned a promotion to deputy managing director, the youngest manager in the Vietnamese banking industry.*
>
> *I have demonstrated my aptitude for client management and relationship building by successfully reconstructing a damaged relationship with a major financial institution and creating the flagship office for this global engagement team. In these capacities, I have consistently proven my ability to mold a diverse team of experts to form cohesive plans and successfully complete projects.*

Stories About Solving Problems

You can also use the storytelling method effectively by using it to tell stories about problems you've solved for your employers. Here are a few examples:

> *My analytical skills have contributed to my ability to solve challenging problems. At FoodAmerica, for example, sales quotas were not tied to financial objectives. I applied my creativity to devising a sales-forecasting system in which order files could be integrated with shipments and invoicing files, and SAS reports could be prepared each morning. I arranged for SAS reports to be e-mailed to each sales unit so all parties could see the sales status daily, ensured that the system tied sales quotas to financial objectives, and added a trend-projection expert system to forecast which products would not make their objectives. This report contributed significantly to the successful startup of the Mighty Macaroni product line.*
>
> *As a consultant at Connor Associates, I have proven myself as a team leader. For example, when the mainframe computer crashed last summer and we lost months of crucial data, I motivated team members to pull extra shifts to duplicate the work in just a few weeks.*

My broad-based background enables me to adapt well to building client relationships. In my current position, for instance, I identified and resolved customer issues with a computer manufacturer, resulting in a $1M contract. Not only did my company win the contract, but its management expressed the organization's satisfaction by providing excellent word-of-mouth promotion of our services to its subsidiaries.

Stories of Other Accomplishments

The story of your past performance shows that you are the best value choice for the employer because you've achieved the same kinds of results the organization seeks, says Robert S. Frey, senior vice president at RS Information Systems, Inc. (RSIS), whom I interviewed for this book. Tell stories that vividly show how you've made a difference for your past employers, as in these examples:

In my most recent music-industry position at BMG, I maintained $1M project budgets and helped boost the record sales of artists such as Clay Aiken, Taylor Hicks, and Carrie Underwood. With great efficiency and productivity, I can oversee budget creation and negotiation for video and photo shoots, hire creative staff, and function as the liaison among artists, their management, and the label.

My immersion into the world of business and finance at Global Financial Advisors has prepared me for business consulting. As a rising adviser who regularly cold-called CEOs and owners of successful Atlanta corporations to persuade them to meet with me, I banked my success on the ability to think creatively, conceptualize on many levels, and communicate crisply. I effectively explained the value my firm could provide and demonstrated my competency in tax, legal, insurance, and investment realms. I helped clients understand complex ideas in simple terms, motivated them to action, and then collaborated with a team of Global associates to implement our ideas.

I have proven my ability to attract and keep customers through the excellent feedback and comments I've received from guests, many of whom have come back and requested me as their server. I've also demonstrated my ability to up-sell by producing total meal sales 15% higher than 80% of servers and increasing my sales by 20% in the past three months. I also won an award for highest beverage sales for a server.

While at Winona State University, I completed numerous programming projects and sharpened my leadership and interpersonal skills. I demonstrated these skills by organizing the 2008 Annual Programmers Dinner, which nearly 300 people attended.

Stories That Reveal Your Personality

These are stories that inspire the employer to want to get to know you better and thus call you in for an interview. They could demonstrate your sense of humor, your work ethic, your compassion, or simply your humanity. They paint a meaningful picture of who you are. Here are a few examples:

I am a builder. I don't mean with hammer and nails, although I enjoy that kind of building, too. At my last employer, I built three organizations that filled specific niches within the parent company. I defined the departments' roles, hired and trained more than 300 team members, and then built the capability. I found it equally rewarding to improve those organizations by adding systems and processes so the teams were recognized for their contribution. I applied my creativity, leadership, and ability to navigate complex and abstract problems.

I admit it. I'm a psychology geek. I have always had an interest in where our behaviors, thoughts, and personalities come from. Since as long ago as I can remember, I would be in the library sifting through the philosophy and psychology shelves. I am an enthusiastic learner and problem solver. I am patient and compassionate and tend to make others feel at ease. I don't judge people based on their successes; rather, I see trials and past experiences as an opportunity for growth and empathy.

I would describe myself as a consistently positive person. My friends sometimes ask me how I can be so energetic. I'm proud of my efforts to pursue my dream of being a clinical dietitian. As you can see from my resume, I changed my career to become a dietitian. I had an interest in food and nutrition since I was a little girl and helped to develop recipes for patients who required food restriction. I strengthened my interest in clinical nutrition as I learned about the field on my own. When I found how clinical nutrition therapy functioned as a preventive medicine, I decided to become a registered dietitian.

I once read that experience working in an insane asylum or as an animal trainer or juggler provides the best background for working as a graphic artist at a design firm. Frankly, I haven't had any of those experiences, but I thrive on the pressure of a fast-paced and intense environment and can juggle several projects simultaneously. My fresh and innovative design skills, along with total Macintosh and PC proficiency, make me the graphic artist you've been looking for.

In your opener, you can also introduce the idea that you will be revealing more of your personality in the letter:

A resume can tell you only the bare bones of my story. This letter is to help you get to know me.

..ories About Your Interest in the Organization

You can tell stories describing your long-term interest in, knowledge of, and admiration for the organization you're targeting. Handle this type of story carefully so that it is framed in terms of how you will benefit the employer—not how working for your long-admired employer will fulfill *your* career dreams. Also be careful about "preaching to the choir"; don't tell the reader things about the company that he or she already knows. Employer-admiration stories could include your experiences as a customer of the organization, such as in the first two examples:

As a seasoned cruise traveler and worker in the hospitality industry, I am well aware of your company's outstanding status as an industry leader. My education and experience in marketing, customer service, sales, information systems, Spanish language, and worldwide travel equip me to enhance the success of Royal Caribbean Cruise Lines.

I have long been an avid consumer of Volkswagen's automobiles. I have a passion for the cars VW produces, and I know I can infuse this same energy into everything I do for you. I would be thrilled to contribute my automotive-design talents to your organization.

More examples of company knowledge/admiration stories:

I have been both an admirer and enthusiast of Birnbaum Investments' many subsidiaries and its ongoing quest to introduce new products that both diversify and capture various aspects of the tourist industry. Birnbaum appears to be the company for future innovation in tourism in Barbados, and I know I can contribute to its continued success.

Having been previously employed at Walt Disney World, I completely understand that customer satisfaction is the main priority in achieving success in the theme-park business. An organization that prides itself on effective recruiting and retaining, training, and managing its employees is best equipped to cater to consumer needs in today's competitive arena.

Parkerson Products' commitment to hiring the best candidates is likely the reason for your first-rate reputation. I am convinced that I am the candidate who can contribute to Parkerson's continued success. That's the reason I am applying for the Product Development Manager position that you advertised on Monster.com.

Having studied Pinnacle's achievements with admiration, I am aware that success at Pinnacle depends on the trainer's ability to convince seminar attendees to enroll in in-depth training programs. I've used my talent for holding an audience's attention to successfully sell household items every summer during my college years. Each summer, I surpassed my sales of the summer before and achieved the highest sales of any collegiate salesperson.

As a lifelong animal lover, I was touched and inspired to read about VetMed's recent success with medications to alleviate arthritis pain in dogs. I am extremely excited that, as a soon-to-be graduate in biology from the University of Tennessee, I am about to make my mark in the world of veterinary pharmaceutical research. I would most like to contribute to the research and development team at VetMed.

This type of story can be quite effective as the opening paragraph in your cover letter by grabbing the employer's attention immediately:

What person interested in working in the rental-car business wouldn't want to bring motivation and talent to the industry leader? My family is extremely brand-loyal to your company, never having even considered renting from any of your competitors. I am very interested in working in this industry, and that's why I'm applying for your manager-trainee vacancy.

Stories Describing Your Fit

You can tell stories that describe how well you fit in with the organization's culture, values, and mission. Frey, who describes himself as a "fact-based story-teller," teaches successful proposal writers to "kiss the customer's mission" (where the customer in this case is the employer), meaning to show that you understand the employer's mission and can demonstrate how it relates to what you can bring to the organization.

In addition to my undergraduate background in business and sales, I have interned with the Sheraton St. Augustine, where I played a key role in selling the five-star hotel's accommodations to journalists and tourists from all over the world. Add to that experience my understanding and appreciation for the sport of golf, and you have the perfect addition to your golf-equipment sales team.

I've spent considerable time researching companies by talking to happy employees. From that research, I know that Stocks Unlimited is a great company to work for, with a friendly environment. It's an organization in which I know I can contribute my skills and talents to their full potential to benefit the firm. I am impressed with your company values; you treat customers the same way you would want to be treated, and I would be proud to be part of your team.

I am excited about your agency's mission "to conserve, protect, and enhance fish and wildlife and their habitats for the continuing benefit of the American people" and I am more than ready to assist those "who work to save endangered and threatened species; conserve migratory birds and inland fisheries; and manage offices and field stations."

Stories About Educational Preparation

New graduates can tell stories of how their education has prepared them for the targeted job. New-grad stories don't have to be about just your classroom education; they can be about your extracurricular activities, leadership experience, sports-team membership, internships, work-study jobs, and the full spectrum of your college experience, as in these examples:

> *Having dedicated a substantial section of my undergraduate thesis to examining tradable permits as a way to regulate carbon emissions, I share the Sierra Club's concern about global warming. As a recent graduate, I am looking to apply my knowledge in the real world.*

> *As a student majoring in accounting at the University of Miami, I have gained significant knowledge in the accounting field. I understand that Baldwin wants to hire someone who can develop an information system to track sales and inventory. I have developed several information systems related to customer orders using Microsoft Access, Microsoft Excel, and Visual Basic.*

> *My recent experience and my classroom knowledge as an accounting major will benefit your company. As director of finance for an organization of 60 individuals, I functioned independently to reconcile bank statements and accounts receivable, bill accounts receivable, prepare accrual journal entries, generate financial statements, create an incentive program, and establish a computerized accounting system. Just as I achieved these goals effectively, I will be productive, proficient, and accurate for your company as well.*

> *Through my internship with Blue Cross/Blue Shield I've fully deployed my marketing skills. I conducted a research study on the motivational behavior of the charitable donors by using communication skills and several business software programs. I have also successfully filled a local grocery store with campus faculty to participate in Celebrity Baggers during my first month as an intern.*

> *As a computer lab assistant I gained invaluable hands-on experience in computer software problem-solving and was promoted to assist professors in coordinating and implementing technical software seminars. My effective interaction with the faculty led to my selection for a highly prestigious position as co-teacher of a university class designed to orient first-year students with college life. I took full responsibility for the theme, syllabus, class discussions, and lectures.*

> *My resume shows that I'm a college student, but I am not a typical undergraduate. I am a highly motivated self-starter. I established a house-painting business to contribute to my college costs. As rush chairman of my fraternity, I was motivated to make my organization the best. While only eight new members were initiated the year before I took office, 22 new members pledged when I held the*

position. Nationals recognized this accomplishment when we received a special award for recruitment.

Stories That Tug the Heartstrings

Emotional stories can be extremely effective, but they must be handled with kid gloves. Although some employers might be touched by the following examples, focus-group participants did not find stories with a "negative" element to be enticing. One participant said, "None of these conveys a positive experience [that] would transfer to their employment and make them a better worker."

I can make a valuable contribution to Maplewood Children's Hospital, based on my past experiences. As a child I spent a lot of time in hospitals, and I vividly remember my feelings in response to the environment. I would like to ensure that children feel as comfortable as possible in an otherwise scary situation.

While working in a summer internship with the Red Cross in Rwanda, I was exposed to human suffering far worse than anything I ever could have imagined. It is out of the sensitivity I acquired toward the misery of oppressed people that I decided to dedicate my career to trying to ease suffering. That is why I am writing to you about the social-worker position you currently have available.

Recently I have spent many long hours at the bedsides of my two brothers, who were both hospitalized for lengthy periods for separate traumas. I thus have personal experience with both short- and long-term patients and the problems they endure while in the hospital.

So, what kinds of "heartstrings" stories are effective? Those that make a more positive connection between the job seeker's heart-tugging experience and his or her ability to do the job, as in these examples:

A particular strength of mine is establishing rapport with patients, often perceiving nonverbal cues that communicate how they are feeling. I am then adept at motivating them to manage or even overcome their dysfunction. I will always remember my 88-year-old patient, Dottie, and the way she smiled with tears in her eyes after my therapy enabled her to write a letter to her first great-grandchild.

Through my experiences, I have gained a deep conviction that improving the quality of early care of children is the best way to improve society. The care that children receive in these early years is pivotal to whether they become pro- or antisocial. The program I developed provided 60 children with appropriate guidance, nutrition, safety, and unconditional love, and had a lasting impact as they developed into adulthood. A much higher percentage of them than is typical for that population are now college bound.

The world of insurance doesn't seem like a breeding ground for the kind of compassion you need in a counselor, but for me it was. When I was in health-insurance claims, a family had lost its home during the Christmas holidays. They lacked the funds to cover their benefit premiums, and their coverage was about to be cancelled. I came up with a payment plan. I also put the father's disability claim on the fast track and collaborated with coworkers to send four big boxes with wrapped Christmas presents to arrive on Christmas Eve.

As the coordinator of a tutoring program for disadvantaged youth, I have developed my ability to motivate and make a difference. I helped a little boy, Jeremy, improve his reading and math grades from Fs to Bs. The same enthusiasm and persuasive skills that aided me in recruiting 115 new volunteers for service projects this year make me a valuable asset for your organization.

Stories to Back Up Your Claims About Yourself

A participant in my focus-group research with recruiters and hiring managers commented that the storytelling cover letters she observed in the study offered "concrete examples of their attribute and skill claims instead of just throwing out the descriptors they think a prospective employer will want to hear."

Six years in restaurant management have taught me every facet of the industry. Through these years our family-owned and -operated company has expanded from a single unit to a nine-restaurant chain. Having been brought up in the business, I've dealt with a diverse array of individuals. I have developed, among other attributes, strong entrepreneurial, interpersonal, and motivational skills, which will contribute to a fruitful and profitable partnership with your company.

My background in sales comes from two summer internships in which I progressed from sales representative to assistant sales manager in the telemarketing department and was hired full-time the next summer as the manager. This experience, coupled with my education, is a surefire asset to your bottom line. My creative and aggressive nature will benefit your company significantly, and I know that I will generate the results you are looking for.

As marketing vice president for GenYX Network, I demonstrated my strategic ability when I successfully positioned our company as a leading Internet-based global distribution firm. I have consistently contributed my marketing management skills while motivating team members, fine-tuning marketing plans and goals, and juggling multiple projects.

The direct functions of my position in the U.S. Navy closely parallel the requirements of your advertised position. I single-handedly managed, tracked, and reported the hospital's financial position, including accounting for income statement and balance-sheet items. I also gained valuable experience in preparing quarterly and annual budgets for the 30-department medical facility.

Diverse professionals comprised the environment in my last workplace, BeautyGem. What I found to be most productive for the operation was to use my unique ability to bridge gaps to develop cooperative working relationships with the staff. I used a judicious mixture of solid interpersonal skills, adaptability to others' needs, and a good sense of humor. I worked hard to deploy these traits with supervisors and colleagues to build an efficient and cohesive office operation that became recognized as highly competent and customer-service oriented.

As a workshop teacher/facilitator and teaching artist for the Lincoln Center Institute for Aesthetic Education program in New York, I consistently applied the philosophy and practice of aesthetic education to my teaching and curriculum development. I have thus created a body of work that is a successful woven quilt of artful investigation, academic enhancement, and integrity in teaching and learning. I have proven my ability to create well-structured units of study that facilitate reflection, integrate all of the arts as teaching tools, engage all learners, remain consistently funded by local arts and state agencies as well as school districts and educational organizations, and enjoy considerable success.

Stories of Your Unique Qualifications

Tell stories that demonstrate your Unique Selling Proposition, or USP. This is an advertising term that refers to the one thing about a product that makes it distinct from all others. Express the one thing that makes you more qualified for this job than anyone else. Your USP story should answer the employer's question: "Why should I hire this person?"

I've played semiprofessional tennis for many years, so I am aware that the equipment a tennis player uses is extremely important. Through my international experience, I have learned that—like the game itself—the tennis industry is highly competitive. Improvements can give a company an edge over its competitors. I am convinced I can provide that quality and competitive advantage because I've done the same during my current position as Marketing Director. I knew that the quality of my employer's marketing department drove the firm's success, so I ensured top-notch performance.

My commitment to building the Hialeah School of Arts as an institution is exemplified by my having contributed to my community as an arts educator, where I have witnessed firsthand that creative learning environments in the arts bring people together, stimulate feelings and emotions, and generate dialogue. I have seen the arts encourage, empower, heal, and restore neighborhoods, communities, and schools, rejuvenating them and bringing them to life.

In my last two editing positions, a 30-gallon trash can in my office has been the destination of 90% of the press releases I received. I could write a book or teach a course on how not to write a news release or mount a publicity campaign. My perspective from the editing desk is why I'm an excellent fit as public-relations director for your organization.

Stories That Capitalize on Networking Contacts

In letters to networking contacts, you can tell a story to remind them of how your paths have crossed in the past.

I enjoyed your recent informative presentation at St. Leo College and was so impressed with your knowledge of trends in pharmaceutical sales. Your talk inspired me to research Hoechst Marion Roussel further. I discovered that my professional demeanor and sales talents would be an excellent match for the world's third-largest drug company. Noticing that Hoechst streamlined its labor force in 2008 demonstrates to me that you emphasize quality rather than quantity, a philosophy that aligns directly with my characteristics. I'd love to tell you more about how my solid academic performance, work ethic, drive, organizational skills, and strong interest in the pharmaceutical industry demonstrate my ability to attain outstanding results for your company.

Back in January, before I relocated to the Bay Area from Ohio, I wrote to you about the possibility of employment with your dynamic company. You generously took the time to reply with an extremely kind letter. You said that with my qualifications, I should have no difficulty finding a job. Having felt such a warm rapport with you from your very nice letter, I thought you might like to know that I've completed my relocation and am ready to enhance the success of a company like yours.

Stories to Explain Unusual or Potentially Negative Situations

It's very difficult to explain in a resume such situations as relocation, extended family-leave time, sabbaticals, illness, disability, unemployment, travel, returning to employment after business ownership, and other employment gaps. The cover letter lends itself much better to these situations, which represent another area for careful handling. You don't want to tell stories that raise more questions than they answer. Nor do you want to call undue attention to an issue that might not be important to the employer. Certainly, do not belabor the special-situation story. Here are some examples of well-executed stories:

When I took maternity leave from my high-powered consulting job with Accenture, I expected to be gone for just a few months. Little did I know that giving birth to a child with autism would not only take me out of the workforce for six years to attend to my son's special needs, but that it would also inspire a whole new career passion as a special-education teacher. Now returning to the workforce with an education degree, I want to combine the communication skills honed through my past consulting experience with the knowledge I've gained as the mother of a special-needs child. I'm well prepared to design and deliver instruction, meet each child's special needs, and ensure that my students reach their full learning potential.

Stories to Explain a Career Change

Although short-term job and career tenures are much more accepted than they used to be, many decision-makers are still suspicious of career changers and want to know what motivates the change. Their mental question is "Why should I consider this career-changing candidate over someone who has always been in this field?" Your story must answer that question by showing your enthusiasm and passion for your new career as well as your transferable skills.

At the very instant I read your ad for a Merchandising Specialist, everything clicked. The description of the job became one with my passion, and I knew the match between me and this job was perfect. I'm ready to make my contribution in an environment where excellence is a given. I accept your challenge; I know I have what it takes, can prove it, and am poised to take my mark and go.

I became a chiropractor because of my desire to help people and make a difference. I strive to do the same with my writing. As a health professional with significant health/medical writing and publishing experience, I have a wealth of skills and talents to offer in the Staff Writer position you currently have open. I am eager to put my attributes to work for you at Healthy Body magazine.

My successes have been frequent and consistent since I joined The Buenger Corporation 10 years ago when it was a $90M company. I played a key role in the organization's growth to $1B. However, I've progressed as far as possible. As a result, I've decided to take on new challenges in a growing firm like yours that could benefit from my large-corporation experience.

Stories That Address Employer Needs

You can tell future stories that address employer needs and challenges and tell how you would address those issues:

When I interviewed Ms. Tranter six months ago to obtain information about a career in yoga instruction, she mentioned that the studio would like to establish a Web presence. I'd like to combine my interest in yoga with my knowledge of Web-page design and HTML programming to help you create a Webmaster position in your studio. I've even sketched out some preliminary ideas on what your Web page might look like, and I'd love to get together and show them to you.

Because I recently assisted in managing one of the convenience stores in your company's chain, I am well acquainted with how to prioritize tasks. I oversaw organization of the employee task list. While corporate headquarters provided the basic structure of the task list, I modified it to meet our store's needs. Now, I'd like to do that for all the corporate stores. Working in "the problem store," as you often called it, I am certainly aware of the difficulties, and I have some ideas about how to solve them.

I understand that Hanover Information Systems deals heavily in telemarketing and database outsourcing. Maintaining a database can be very expensive for a company, and outsourcing this task can sometimes be more efficient. I am confident that I can help increase the company's productivity by creating optimal ways to maintain the databases.

Do's and Don'ts for Storytelling Cover Letters

Even if you are taking the innovative step of integrating stories into your cover letters, you still need to follow the guidelines of good cover letter writing. Here are guidelines for cover letters, especially those that include stories.

Cover Letter Do's

First here are the basic ideas to keep in mind when writing cover letters.

Do Make the Letter as Concise as Possible

Employers are not spending as much time as they used to reading cover letters. Ideally, your letter should be about four paragraphs, and one of those should tell a story.

Do Make It Reader-Friendly

Even the narrative cover letter has succumbed to employers' insatiable hunger for bullet points, which are a nice way to break up blocks of type and make your letter easy to read. Focus-group participants responded well to the sample shown on page 102, which includes both a story and a bulleted section. It's also possible to tell a story in bullet form, as in this example:

In my four years as sales manager of a leading medical-supply distributor in Redwood City, I directed the sales and marketing of the company's line of breathing apparatuses. During that time:

- *I led the sales team in tripling annual billings, from $3M to nearly $11M.*
- *I contributed to a five-fold increase in company profits, from $150K in 2001 to $785K for the fiscal year ending in 2008.*

- *I guided a 250% increase in the number of accounts in our group's sales territory.*

The success I've had here and elsewhere in 15 years of selling is not a coincidence or attributable to luck or magic. My sales prowess results from a natural ability to analyze a marketing/selling situation and deliver an innovative program that leaves the competition behind.

Use tables as another way to tell a story in a user-friendly format. Remember Mathias Carroll's Project Highlights Resume Addendum from chapter 4? An alternative to using the full addendum is to extract three or four storied key projects and use them in the middle of your cover letter, as in the example on page 101.

Do Make Your Stories Specific and Quantify Results Whenever Possible

It's always easier for the reader to picture you succeeding on the job when you describe a specific situation. In addition, employers are always attracted to numbers that indicate results.

Do Use Compelling Stories

Stories for the sake for storytelling won't get you far. Be sure the stories you include in your cover letter will grab the reader.

Do Tell Relevant Stories

Tell only the stories that are relevant to the employer's requirements, the problems you can solve, and the results you can achieve. If the relevance isn't immediately obvious from your story, help the reader make the connection by pointing out the skills and qualifications the story illustrates. For example:

The exceptional organizational abilities and detail orientation I deployed to set up photo shoots are directly applicable to the skills needed to plan and coordinate events. I can enhance your profitability by prospecting new business opportunities, strategizing communication initiatives, successfully managing client relationships, delivering presentations, and much more.

Do Use Some of the Employer's Messages and Language

Go to the employer's Web site or pick up print publications about the organization. Pick out buzzwords and phrases. Play these back to the employer in your story. Employers who read language-mirroring stories conclude that the job seeker "gets it." Decision-makers love to see the organization's own words reflected back to them. Both of the following examples take their inspiration from employer Web sites. In the first example, the site stated that the company was staffed by people who could, like Superman, "leap tall buildings in a single bound."

I'm ready to leap tall buildings in a single bound. Knowing that you surround yourself with people who care passionately about their work, I'm here to tell you that I am passionate about working for Henderson Partners. My solid experience in serving the administrative needs of busy offices in fast-paced environments enables me to make a significant contribution to the Administrative Assistant/Receptionist position you are currently advertising.

The description of The Limited at your Web site leads me to believe that your company and I share a philosophy about creativity, fashion, and customer service. That's why I'm eager to contribute my experience in interacting with all kinds of people, combined with a genuine passion for fashion and a tremendous admiration for The Limited, in an Associate capacity, particularly with Express.

Cover Letter Don'ts

Now here are some things to avoid.

Don't Neglect the "Storyline" in the Rest of the Letter

Even if only one paragraph in your letter is in story form, try to integrate the story's theme throughout your letter and tie together the letter by briefly referring back to the story in your final paragraph. See the sample letters starting on page 100.

Don't Write Your Autobiography

Telling a story doesn't mean describing your entire career; that's what your resume is for. For example, the following paragraph is too long and contains too many ideas that are not only unconnected to the job the writer seeks as a computer programmer, but are also disconnected from each other:

For nearly three years I have been a student computer technician for Academic Computing Services at Bucknell University. I am responsible for the repair and maintenance of all faculty, staff, and computer lab machines on campus. My duties also include the maintenance of our network and servers. Parallel with these responsibilities, I am also a lab supervisor for Academic Computing Services. I am also responsible for designing and maintaining several of Bucknell's home pages for the World Wide Web, experience that has provided me with a detailed knowledge of the HTML programming language. In August 2009, I will complete my bachelor's degree in philosophy. My liberal arts background has equipped me with exemplary communication skills. I have taken several math and computer science courses in my college career. My mathematics background includes trigonometry, statistics, calculus I and II, linear algebra, logic, and discrete math. I have also taken several computer science courses. In these courses, I work with Assembly, Pascal, C/C++, and several other languages. I am currently programming using C/C++ in the Windows NT and Windows XP environments.

Here's how that rambling paragraph might be rewritten to tell a better story that relates more closely to specific skills:

> *Having overseen repair and maintenance of all faculty, staff, and computer lab machines on the Bucknell University campus for nearly three years also qualifies me well for your advertised Help Desk Analyst/Programmer position. I also maintain our network and servers. My experience as a lab supervisor bolsters my management skills.*
>
> *The strong liberal-arts background I've attained through my upcoming bachelor's degree in philosophy (August 2009) has equipped me with the exemplary communication skills your organization requires.*
>
> *I combine both my HTML programming skills and communication talents in designing and maintaining several Bucknell Web pages. I offer a strong math background and the diverse programming skills you need through my coursework in Assembly, Pascal, C/C++, and several other languages in the Windows NT and Windows XP environments.*

Don't Overlook Story Cues in Want Ads

The principle here is similar to the language-mirroring described in the preceding section. In his book *Don't Send a Resume,* Jeffrey Fox calls the best letters written in response to want ads "boomerang letters" because they "fly the want ad words—the copy—back to the writer of the ad." In employing what Fox calls "a compelling sales technique," he advises letter writers to "flatter the person who wrote the ad with your response letter. Echo the author's words and intent. Your letter should be a mirror of the ad." Fox notes that when the recipient reads such a letter, the thought process will be "This person seems to fit the description."

In the following example, the employer playfully wrote in the want ad that the prospective new hire should have the characteristics of 1980s TV character "MacGyver," who was highly resourceful in dealing with sticky situations with minimal tools:

> *MacGyver to the rescue! Armed with my trusty toothpick and duct tape—actually my exceptional facility with hand-coded, highly maintainable HTML—I am poised to create high-quality, totally usable Web pages for your clients. My three years of experience with Web-development projects make me exactly the kind of value-added employee you need in the Content Architect position you are advertising. My solid communication skills, along with total proficiency in all the areas you require, will enable me to make a significant contribution to your team.*

Don't Forget Good Cover Letter Guidelines

Many resources for writing solid cover letters are available and listed at the end of this book. You can find a handy checklist at www.quintcareers.com/cover_letter_checklist.html.

Sample Story-Based Cover Letters

To give you some ideas about what a full cover letter might look like with stories contained within it, here are three sample cover letters that each take a different approach to incorporating stories.

Dear [specific named individual]:

My deep-rooted passion for travel abroad will enable me to serve your company well as an international consultant based in Japan. I must confess that I have always had a passion for international travel and a curiosity for investigating other cultures. As a child, my grandparents filled my stamp collection with brightly colored stamps, souvenirs from their travels. I remember being so captivated by my treasure chest of stamps that I vowed to visit these places one day. I was nearly 13 during my first overseas adventure, and since then I have pursued several adventures abroad, including extended trips to Japan, the United Kingdom, and Europe, and a three-month internship with a consulting company in Portugal.

As a new graduate educated in international trade and consulting, I can offer your company expertise that will meet or even exceed your needs in export/import. My background has prepared me for multiple, diverse challenges in communicating with international clients, paying strong attention to detail, and producing essential documentation.

My hard work, professionalism, and dedication to employer success have resulted in significant accolades and increased responsibilities. My superb organizational skills, firm understanding of global trade regulations, and awareness of the bottom line proved highly beneficial in my recent internship. Additionally, I can bring the following experiences and skills to this position:

- Ability to manage post-trade follow-up on delivery, quality specification, regulatory issues, reorders and changes in orders.
- Experience in traveling and living internationally and collaborating with individuals from many cultures with varied communication skills, work habits, and expectations.
- Strong work ethic combined with the ability to perform in high-pressure, fast-paced environments with long hours.
- Fluency in Mandarin Chinese, Taiwanese, Japanese, and English.
- Excellent computer skills.

My education in management and foreign trade—as well as my strong decision-making, problem-solving, and action-driven leadership skills combined with my overseas experiences—makes me an excellent choice for the consulting position you are advertising. My childhood dream of global travel has transformed me into a worldly consultant for your firm. I plan to contact you to set up a personal interview at your convenience. Thank you in advance for your consideration.

Sincerely,

Yi Chan

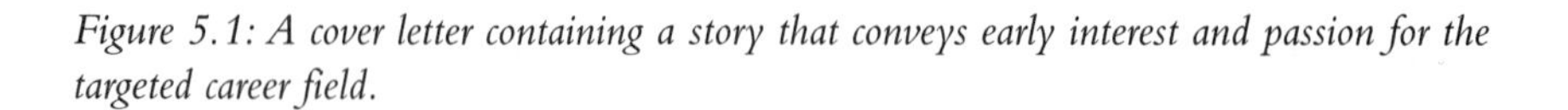

Figure 5.1: A cover letter containing a story that conveys early interest and passion for the targeted career field.

MATHIAS CARROLL

91110 Forest Dr., Apt 126, Houston, TX 77096 ◆ Phone: 713-555-5555
E-mail: carroll_m@hotmail.com

Date

Specific name of recipient
Company
Address
Address

Dear [specific named individual]:

My leadership experience in multiple roles in financial project management and profitability maximization, along with my ability to deliver high performance, identify me as a powerful, cross-functional contributor equipped to perform proficiently as a Project Director for [name of company].

More than 10 years of accomplishment in project management in a financial setting have provided me with a comprehensive expertise that ensures my continuing career success. In me you will find someone who applies unusual dedication and self-motivation, and offers the focus, drive, and leadership skills to excel seamlessly in a high-pressure, fast-paced environment. The project results below represent just a small sampling of what I can achieve for your firm:

Project	Challenge	Action & Results
Enhancements to External Communication to Clients	Customer correspondence was inconsistent with established brand image and noncompliance risk existed.	First to visualize and implement new use for established internal customer setup system. Designed/implemented automated customer letter trigger to ensure consistent brand image and that important correspondence is sent to client while contributing to operational efficiency; became the standard for all departmental products.
ACH Risk Initiative	Risk initiative designed to automate funding of ACH files and broaden credit policies to enable more customer penetration while managing risk.	First in market. Developed strategies to address gap in training and simplify a complicated process. Exceeded expectations and goals of project, garnering executive leadership praise on implementation success. Market studies showed lead in positioning and also exposed larger customer segment to product traditionally targeted for large corporate clients.
Banking Bundles	Initiative to create new product that included offering of products not traditionally offered to small-business clients.	First in market, exposing 200+ sales force to new products. Simplified product offering and backroom setup for seamless implementation; sales steadily increased, growing by 10% monthly.

My former employers can attest to my ability to deploy highly intricate strategic initiatives with precision and clarity. I'm intelligent and goal-oriented, and can quickly synthesize the mission and nuances of your organization and make an immediate, tangible contribution.

I am the complete package, and I am confident in my ability to consistently exceed company goals and deliver the same kind of extraordinary results to [name of organization] that I have in my many projects. I would greatly appreciate the opportunity to meet with you to discuss the contribution I can make to your organization. I will contact you soon to arrange an interview. Should you wish to speak to me before then, you can reach me using the contact information atop this letter. I thank you for considering me and look forward to meeting with you.

Sincerely,

Mathias Carroll

Figure 5.2: A cover letter with Challenge-Action-Results stories within a table.

Date
Specific name of recipient
Company
Address
Address

Dear [specific named individual]:

My comprehensive technology optimization experience in planning, building, integrating, and deploying IT initiatives makes me exactly the kind of value-added employee you need to capably contribute to the ongoing success of your organization. My self-motivation and multitasking skills along with proficiency in a wide variety of hardware, applications, and networking protocols will enable me to significantly contribute to the [name of organization] team. Specifically, I can offer the following to your bottom line:

- The experience that makes me a value-added and innovative solution-provider—yet, at the same time, a down-to-earth, hands-on, hard worker with finely honed troubleshooting skills;
- A solid and extensive understanding of the systems technology that drives today's businesses as well as a broad understanding of business and productivity principles that effectively and seamlessly integrate technology with bottom-line profitability;
- The flexibility, adaptability, and solutions-driven mindset that enables me to delve into complex systems functionality issues.

Frequently called upon to provide technical engineering support for implementing and integrating applications to optimize systems, I have consistently deployed my skills to provide attainable solutions. One of my most rewarding accomplishments was stabilizing a Fortune 500 company's infrastructure by examining areas where the outages were occurring and then generating buy-in for implementing a preventive-maintenance schedule that proactively rebooted systems during scheduled downtimes and performing database cleaning during scheduled outages to reduce unplanned outages. My plan reduced the number of high-severity incidents from multiple instances a week to less than one per quarter.

I look forward to providing superior systems-engineering expertise to manage and optimize your service operations, and I am eager to assist with growing and mentoring your highly skilled work team.

I'd like to meet with you to discuss adding value to your organization—contributing systems stability, incident reduction, and more—as I've done for my previous employers. I'll contact you in the near future to arrange a meeting. Should you wish to reach me before then, please contact me at (555) 555-5555 or jwinters@email.com. I appreciate your consideration.

Sincerely,

Janet Winters

Figure 5.3: A cover letter containing a story that describes a specific accomplishment.

Summary

Stories can significantly enhance your cover letters, which are an even better medium for stories than resumes. Cover letters should always be interesting for the reader, rather than dry and formulaic. Stories provide a way to enliven your letters. You can communicate a wide variety of information through stories that will enhance your connection with the employer.

CHAPTER 6

PORTFOLIOS THAT TELL A STORY

A career portfolio, also known as an employment portfolio or a skills port folio, can be a versatile workhorse in job search storytelling. As you'll see in this chapter, a portfolio can help you tell your story in a number of ways:

- The simple act of creating a portfolio enables you to get to know your own stories better and develop new stories.
- An online portfolio can entice employers to contact you, in part, by presenting your success stories in an appealing manner.
- A print portfolio serves as a tangible and visual guide to describing your accomplishments in narrative form in job interviews.
- Either type of portfolio serves as a repository for all of your critical job search materials.

Paulson and Paulson write that "a portfolio tells a story. It is the story of knowing. Knowing about things.... Knowing oneself.... Knowing an audience.... Portfolios are [people's] own stories of what they know, why they believe they know it, and why others should be of the same opinion."

The Portfolio Explained

What is a career portfolio? It's a job hunting tool that job seekers develop to give employers a picture that is much more complete than a cover letter and resume: experience, education, accomplishments, skill sets, and potential contribution to the employer's organization.

In a time when many employers are skeptical of the claims job seekers make on their resumes concerning their experiences and contributions, a career portfolio can be just the tool to use to substantiate your stories and enhance your telling them.

Portfolio Formats

The two main delivery systems for career portfolios are print—a physical portfolio typically contained in a binder—and online—a virtual portfolio that resides on the Web. Each is best used at a distinct time in the job search. An online portfolio is most useful for enabling employers to find you online and for enticing them to invite you for an interview through its media-rich presentation. A print portfolio's most effective use is once you are in the interview. It enables you to show the interviewer visible examples of your success stories, especially in response to specific interview questions.

Whether print or online, career portfolios should be filled with artifacts and information that clearly show your accomplishments and tell the story of why you are the ideal candidate for the position you are seeking.

What to Include in a Portfolio

In research with career experts conducted by career-development Web site Quintessential Careers, one respondent said of portfolio content, "I want to see items or artifacts that represent that individual and tell a story of accomplishments that relate to the job in question." Another added that "the portfolio is an opportunity for the candidate to offer 'proof' of what is on the resume. Emphasis should be on skills, abilities, and accomplishments. The portfolio can be an opportunity for a 'show and tell' experience elaborating on the work history. Special skills could be highlighted."

Items that a job seeker could consider including in a career portfolio:

- Table of contents, index
- Resumes (traditional and text version)
- Career goals/objectives/summary
- Professional philosophy/mission statement
- List of accomplishments
- Success stories/narratives
- Project summary reports
- Resume addenda, such as those described in chapter 4
- Samples of work, writing, and reports
- Performance reviews
- Leadership experience
- Transcripts, degrees, licenses, and certifications

- Awards and honors
- Volunteer/community service
- Professional-development activities
- Professional memberships
- Letters of recommendation, commendation, kudos
- Reference list
- Clippings about you from newspapers, magazines, company newsletters, and other publications
- Photos of you in action in the workplace
- Answers to common job interview questions
- Research you have conducted on the company. This information provides a great opening in an interview to tell a story while showing the employer the research materials in your portfolio about your (positive) experience with the organization's product or service.

Craig Wortmann of WisdomTools, Inc., describes a "win book," a central archive for your collection of accomplishments-oriented artifacts, especially those providing positive feedback about your work. While Wortmann suggests pasting the items into a book, a folder or box is the best way to store these materials until you are ready to create or update your portfolio. Wortmann recommends archiving such items as notes on daily conversations and meetings, ideas about strategy and best practices, stories of how you've impacted the organization, to-do lists, notes you've kept on the professional development of the team members who report to you, and illustrations and models that apply to your industry. Following Wortmann's advice, I kept all the calendar pages from the large desk-pad calendars I used to plan my workload because notations of meetings I attended and projects I worked on reminded me of accomplishments.

Finally, Wortmann suggests going through your artifacts and constructing a table, which he calls a Story Matrix, about them. The columns list the most important skills for the job you seek. The rows of the table document successes, failures, fun, and legends. See an illustration of this Story Matrix in Wortmann's article at http://wisdomtools.com/documents/Beyond_Bits_and_Bullets.pdf.

Career experts generally advise you not to include information about family, friends, pets, parties, hobbies, health, marital status, and religious, political, and social affiliations. Opinions are mixed about including photos in portfolios.

Some experts feel they humanize the candidate; others caution that including your photo can expose you to discrimination. But even if you decide to forgo portrait-type photos of yourself, incorporating workplace photos that show you on the job in such situations as collaborating on team projects and winning awards can help you tell your story.

Developing Stories Through Portfolio Preparation

Job seekers learn more about their own stories and qualifications by preparing a career portfolio, thus boosting their confidence and preparing them for job interviews regardless of whether they actually use the portfolio in the interview, according to the Quintessential Careers study.

Creating a portfolio generates self-confidence and self-knowledge of your skills and strengths. In a sense, when you create the portfolio, you are constructing your story. You give yourself an opportunity to review and interpret your accomplishments and achievements in a way that those who don't create portfolios don't experience. By using your print portfolio as a resource to prepare for interviews, you become more comfortable and confident in telling your story. Even if you don't get the opportunity to present your portfolio to the employer, remembering your success stories through the visual cues you absorbed while reviewing it will help your interview performance.

Here is a sample story by one of my former students, Billy Houghton, published in his online portfolio at www.stetson.edu/~whoughto/personal/bio.html. The personal revelations in this story, especially about religion, are certainly not for everyone. Revealing religious and political affiliations is always risky in the job search because employers who are not like-minded may exclude you. The story also doesn't particularly focus on professional and business skills. Still, it is a charming, engaging story that humanizes Billy and could well entice an employer to get to know him better. Or Billy could instead use the story as a starting place for getting to know himself and creating more professional stories—perhaps about the persistence and competitive drive he has developed as a golfer or the values he's learned from his close-knit family.

> *I was born and raised in Fort Myers, Florida, and I am a 20-year-old student at Stetson University. I am a finance major as well as a business law and MIS minor. This January I am planning on running in my first marathon in Orlando, so I'm spending a lot of time training right now. I also enjoy lifting and working out, but my most enjoyable sport is definitely golf. We get the great blessing of playing Victoria Hills every day, which is going to be hard to beat once I graduate. Golf is by far my most passionate sport, and I enjoy the challenges I face on the course, learning how to tackle the obstacles I face. Aside from sports, I do a lot*

with FCA (Fellowship of Christian Athletes) and ministry. God has opened my eyes to the greatness of Jesus Christ and I am thankful to know Him as my Lord and Savior. I enjoy leading worship at FCA and I am blessed to be a part of a great campus ministry!

My family is also from Fort Myers, going back four generations. I am fortunate to know my grandparents very well, on either side of my family. Even more, I have known three great-grandparents well, who have also lived in Fort Myers. On my mother's side, my great-grandparents spent their lives in Belton, South Carolina, but recently moved down to Fort Myers. They have lived with my grandparents for the past two years. My great-grandfather (Bill McGill) recently passed away, but his wife Fannie is still living. She is a great lady, and I am lucky to know her. I also knew my great-grandmother on my father's side. Her name was Charlie-Bell Murray, but I called her Nannie. She was an amazing lady. One of my best memories with Nannie was looking forward to playing Skip-Bo with her. She was always a competitor, and we had a great time together.

Growing up in Fort Myers has been great for me, and I really enjoy life there! I have a great group of friends, and most of the time we either play golf or go out in the boat.

I have a great set of parents and an awesome sister. My dad works as a consultant (Globalnet Communications) and my mom is a microbiologist. Dad enjoys working on his 1970 GTO, and my mom plays USTA 4.5 tennis; she is quite good on the courts! My sister recently graduated from Stetson, where she played softball for two years. She began her college career at University of Florida, playing softball as well, but transferred to Stetson her junior year. All in all, we have a great time together and one of our most enjoyable things to do is grill shrimp and grouper together!

If you have any questions, please feel free to send me an email! Thanks for visiting my site!

Another former student named Agnes tells in her online portfolio at www.dbindb.com/agnes/about.html the poignant story of growing up in Communist Poland, inspired by her determined mother, a breast-cancer survivor, to overcome adversity and work hard to achieve her dreams.

A Web Portfolio Makes Your Story Accessible 24/7

One of the hot topics in job hunting relates to the degree to which recruiters and human resources professionals are using search engines such as Google to see what kind of information is available online about candidates. According to a study by ExecuNet, almost 80 percent of recruiters said they conducted

Internet searches on candidates, and more than a third of them have eliminated candidates based on the results of the search.

A professional resume writer in the Quintessential Careers study said, "I believe the importance of an online presence for job seekers parallels the importance of an online presence for companies 10 years ago, when the Web was first gaining traction. In time, as with Web sites for companies, an online presence will be second nature to job seekers; the presence is like a resume but better, as it continues to promote them 24/7 and can provide more and better information than the traditional constraints of a paper resume allow."

A personal Web site with a portfolio provides a way to ensure that your name will pop up in an Internet search when an employer enters keywords corresponding to someone with your skills and background, manage what people see when they search for your name online, and put your best foot forward to employers. Employers may find your portfolio on their own while searching the Web for candidates. Or you may refer an employer to your portfolio after cold-calling about vacancies or responding to an ad, thus giving the employer the opportunity to review the portfolio before or after interviewing you. Having a portfolio presence on the Web shows employers that you are technically savvy, open to new trends, and poised on the cutting edge.

TIP: For extra visibility, buy a domain name that includes your name (for example: maryhhansen.com). It's an important and inexpensive thing to do. You can buy a domain name for around $10 a year at sites such as godaddy.com.

Consider the story you'd like to convey with your site and portfolio. Try this exercise: Think of three major trends or themes that have spanned your career and have been ongoing patterns; for example, you've always been a people person. Convey this story consistently throughout your portfolio.

A portfolio published on the Web enables you to include links to all kinds of items that tell more about your story and support it with evidence of your accomplishments. For example, you can link to writing samples, graphic-design samples, ad campaigns, photographs, PowerPoint presentations, reports, graphs, charts, lists of accomplishments and awards, executive summaries, case studies, testimonials, project deliverables, and even multimedia items such as video and sound clips that employers can access 24/7.

Be sure your Web site and portfolio look professional and avoid unbusinesslike content. There's a fine line between opening enough of a window into your personality to intrigue a prospective employer and turning a visitor off with inappropriate family photos or off-color humor. Still, you'll often find some elements in a Web portfolio that you wouldn't find in a typical resume—accessible language and, as mentioned, sometimes photos of the candidate, which facilitate a sort of virtual networking through which employers can get to know prospective employees better. The portfolio provides a great opportunity for the candidate and employer to build rapport before an interview even takes place.

At the Web site of the personal branding experts at Brandego (http://brandego.com/samples.php), see some portfolio samples that not only tell success stories but also illustrate the branding described in chapter 8. Refer to that chapter for more exploration of building an online presence through telling your personal branding story.

Using Your Print Portfolio to Tell Your Story in Interviews

You can use a print portfolio in job interviews to showcase a point and illustrate the depth of your skills and experience using storytelling. Presenting part of your portfolio is especially useful at the beginning of the interview, particularly in your storied response to the "tell me about yourself" request.

Example:

> Interviewer: *Tell me about yourself.*
>
> Keith: *After graduating from high school, I began attending the local community college. After about a year I became very bored. I was also very lonely because all of my friends had moved away. I realized that I was growing restless and could no longer focus on my classes. I decided that it was time for a change. I withdrew from all my classes and gave all of my clothing to my friends and the local thrift store. [opening his portfolio to a page of colorful travel photos] I bought a one-way ticket to Hong Kong and broke the news to my parents, who understandably were dumbfounded. Within two weeks of making my decision, I was on my way to Hong Kong. I had no plan and no luggage except for a small school backpack. [pointing to photos that illustrate his adventures] For nine months I traveled around Southeast Asia and experienced adventure after adventure—from trekking in the Himalayas to appearing in a Thai movie and sitcom [pointing to photos that show those specific experiences], I experienced more than most people experience in a lifetime, all at the age of 18. Looking back on the whole experience, I still find it hard to believe that I did it. I now know that I am capable of doing just about anything I put my mind to and that I have no problem with stepping out of my comfort zone.*

Interviewer: *Are you a team player?*

Lani: *Yes. Let me show you an example in my portfolio. I was project coordinator for the Arizona State Lupus Control Program, and Arizona had never had a lupus grant. A $60,000 grant (including my salary) funded the 25-member advisory committee I formed to write a Lupus state plan. My vision was to integrate a team of professionals and heal lupus in Arizona by interweaving Western medicine with Eastern and Native American medicine. [opens portfolio and shows photos of diverse individuals collaborating with each other] I gathered, interviewed, and invited physicians, Native American healers, chiropractors, Reiki masters, orthopedic surgeons, the chief of military medicine physicians, senators, private researchers, professors, and physicians to join together to heal Arizonans by integrating healing and medicine [shows copy of the Lupus state plan]. I led the writing of the plan, which was distributed to the legislature and the U.S Congress. Our U.S. senator wrote a letter [shows copy of letter] praising the plan's philosophy.*

Use your portfolio to tell stories in response to questions about specific problems and work situations, answering the questions while showcasing corresponding work from your portfolio. "The portfolio can be used more to highlight an example of a topic or question in the interview," states a career expert from the Quintessential Careers research. "The candidate should think of the individual parts of the portfolio as examples in the interview, rather than trying to incorporate the whole portfolio to be worked in somewhere. I think of the portfolio in the interview as a teaser. Once you pull out something as an example, then I might wonder, 'what else do you have in that portfolio?' Then I want to definitely see it, or at least more of it."

You can also use your portfolio to wrap up the job interview by offering to show more of your work so that the interviewer can learn more about you. Introduce the portfolio by saying something like "I noticed we didn't discuss the project-management skills that you mentioned in your job posting. Would you like me to show you one of the biggest projects I managed?" Then, tell the story of the project as you illustrate the narrative with your portfolio.

Linking Interview Questions to Portfolio Artifacts

Be proactive in presenting your portfolio to interviewers in response to interview questions. This section provides examples of interview questions that might prompt you to use your portfolio in a story that illustrates the topic of the interviewer's question. You can begin your responses to many interview questions by saying, "Let me show you an example in my portfolio of exactly what you're asking about...." Don't overdo it, though; time is often tight for interviews, so limit your portfolio presentations to responses that illustrate your best and most relevant skills and accomplishments.

Questions About Your Education

In response to the following types of questions, show examples of school projects with real-world applications, as well as other evidence of student success (transcripts, awards, descriptions of extracurricular activities, and so on).

- How has your college experience prepared you for this career?
- How will the academic program and coursework you've taken benefit your career?
- Which college classes or subjects did you like best? Why?
- Are you the type of student for whom conducting independent research has been a positive experience?
- Describe the type of professor that has created the most beneficial learning experience for you.
- Do you think that your grades are an indication of your academic achievement?
- Give an example of how you applied knowledge from previous coursework to a project in another class.
- What are your standards of success in school? What have you done to meet these standards?

Questions About Career Choice

In response to the following types of questions, show artifacts representing the origins of your interest in your career, perhaps through a class, organization, project, or person.

- What influenced you to choose this career?
- Why did you decide to seek a position in this field?

Questions About Your Goals

In response to the following types of questions, show artifacts that demonstrate the skills and accomplishments that are foundational to reaching your goals.

- What will it take to attain your goals, and what steps have you taken toward attaining them?
- Describe what you've accomplished toward reaching a recent goal for yourself.

- Give me an example of an important goal that you had set in the past and tell me about your success in reaching it.

Questions About Your Skills

This section covers the most important skills that you might be asked to substantiate in an interview.

General Skills

In response to the following type of question, show artifacts that demonstrate the skills and accomplishments that are keys to success in your chosen career.

- What do you think it takes succeed in this career?

Teamwork Skills

In response to the following type of question, show artifacts that illustrate successful team projects.

- How would you describe yourself in terms of your ability to work as a member of a team?

Problem-Solving Skills

In response to the following types of questions, point to artifacts that illustrate your problem-solving skills.

- Tell me about a major problem you recently handled. Were you successful in resolving it?
- Give me a specific example of a time when you used good judgment and logic in solving a problem.
- Describe a time when you were faced with problems or stresses that tested your coping skills.
- What steps do you follow to study a problem before making a decision?
- We can sometimes identify a small problem and fix it before it becomes a major problem. Give an example(s) of how you have done this.
- Describe a specific problem you solved for your employer or professor. How did you approach the problem? What role did others play? What was the outcome?

Multitasking Skills

In response to the following types of questions, show two or three diverse artifacts that illustrate your adaptability and multitasking skills.

- By providing examples, convince me that you can adapt to a wide variety of people, situations, and environments.
- Tell of some situations in which you have had to adjust quickly to changes over which you had no control. What was the impact of the change on you?
- Describe a situation that required a number of things to be done at the same time. How did you handle it? What was the result?
- Tell me about a time you had to handle multiple responsibilities. How did you organize the work you needed to do?
- Describe the system you use for keeping track of multiple projects. How do you track your progress so that you can meet deadlines? How do you stay focused?

Decision-Making Skills

In response to the following types of questions, present artifacts that illustrate your decision-making skills.

- Give an example of a time in which you had to be relatively quick in coming to a decision.
- Give me an example of a time you had to make an important decision. How did you make the decision? How does it affect you today?
- Tell me about a time when you had to make a decision but didn't have all the information you needed.

Communication Skills

In response to the following type of question, show a project sample with the accompanying piece of written communication.

- Describe a time when you had to use your written communication skills to get across an important point.

Presentation Skills

In response to the following types of questions, walk the interviewer through the presentation, perhaps showing the PowerPoint slides you developed, visual aids you used, and photos of the actual presentation.

- What has been your experience in giving presentations? What has been your most successful experience in speech making?
- Describe the most significant or creative presentation that you have had to complete.

Project Management Skills

In response to the following types of questions, show project deliverables, timelines, photos, praise from supervisors, and any awards you've earned.

- Recall a time when you were assigned what you considered to be a complex project. Specifically, what steps did you take to prepare for and finish the project? Were you happy with the outcome? What one step would you have done differently if given the chance?
- What was the most complex assignment you have had? What was your role?
- Describe some projects or ideas (not necessarily your own) that were implemented or carried out successfully primarily because of your efforts.

Creativity Skills

In response to the following types of questions, present artifacts that show your creativity and innovation.

- Have you found any ways to make school or a job easier or more rewarding or to make yourself more effective?
- Give me a specific example of something you did that helped build enthusiasm in others.
- Give me an example of a time you had to persuade other people to take action. Were you successful?
- Give me a specific example of a time when you sold your supervisor or professor on an idea or concept. How did you proceed? What was the result?

- Tell me about a time when you came up with an innovative solution to a challenge your company/class/organization was facing. What was the challenge? What role did others play?

Questions About Your Accomplishments

In response to the following types of questions, take the employer through a success story illustrated in your portfolio.

- How do you determine or evaluate success? Give me an example of one of your successful accomplishments.
- What has been your most rewarding accomplishment?
- What is the most significant contribution you made to the company during a past job?

Questions About Your Qualifications and Characteristics

In response to the following types of questions, show artifacts that demonstrate the qualifications and personal characteristics that will enable you to succeed in your chosen career.

- Do you have the qualifications and personal characteristics necessary for success in your chosen career?
- What quality or attribute do you feel will most contribute to your career success?

Questions About Why They Should Hire You

In response to the following type of question, show artifacts that illustrate your best selling points and why the interviewer should hire you over any other candidate.

- Given the investment our company will make in hiring and training you, can you give us a reason to hire you?

Questions About Your Company Knowledge

In response to the following types of questions, show the interviewer the research you've compiled on the organization. Obviously, you need to tailor this portfolio section to each employer you interview with. This intelligence-gathering will demonstrate that you've done your homework. If you're asked about suggestions for the organization, you can be prepared to point to your research as you share a few ideas for the employer.

- Tell me what you know about our company.
- Why did you decide to seek a position in this company?
- What suggestions do you have for our organization?

Questions About Exceptional Effort

In response to the following type of question, show an artifact that illustrates exceptional effort.

- Tell me about a time when you had to go above and beyond the call of duty in order to get a job done.

Summary

A career portfolio is a job search storytelling tool on many levels. It enables you to develop your stories as you develop the portfolio, and tell your stories in interviews, enhancing them with the rich illustration of your portfolio artifacts. A Web portfolio entices employers to invite you to an interview by telling your story more comprehensively than a mere resume can.

Randall S. Hansen, Ph.D., contributed to this chapter.

CHAPTER 7

Interviews That Tell a Story

Unlike with resumes, cover letters, networking, and portfolios, the integration of story with employment interviewing has been a well-known and highly touted technique for some time. Career author Frank Traditi, in the article "Why Storytellers Get the Job They Want," recommends telling success stories about overcoming significant challenges.

In focus-group research conducted for this book, participants were asked to evaluate a set of story-based interview responses compared with responses that did not contain stories. Participants who preferred the storied responses had the following comments:

- The story responses presented more information.
- The story responses incorporated the job seeker's personal style into handling business.
- The job seeker who gave the story responses communicated/sold herself in a very positive light.
- The storytelling respondent was the more memorable candidate since "I would have had more time to get to know her through her answers and the time I spent with her."
- The story responses were quite the opposite of those without stories in that the storytelling job seeker expressed herself in a "colorful" manner. She incorporated into her stories terms that employers like to hear during an interview—reliable, trustworthy, loyal, team player, creative.
- The storytelling responses allowed the interviewer to see how the job seeker took on a task and handled it.
- The nonstory responses, although concise, did .not impress upon the interviewer how the job seeker could benefit the organization, nor did they provide a sense of his personal style and ways of handling the day-to-day situations that may arise.

The one caution these participants had about the storied responses was to make them as concise as possible and not too wordy. Participants wanted details—but not too many. "Although one does not want to go overboard when talking about [oneself]," one participant said, "it is important to incorporate the needs of the employer with the qualities of the person being interviewed."

Using Stories in Behavioral Interviews

Typically, career experts advise candidates to respond to behavioral-interview questions with stories. "Your examples are best told through a story format," writes Carole Martin in *Boost Your Interview I.Q.* "The more interesting and relevant the story is, the more the interviewer will want to hear further examples."

And just what is a behavioral interview? Developed by industrial psychologists in the 1970s, it's a behavior-based interview approach that increasing numbers of employers are using to screen job candidates. The premise behind behavioral interviewing is that the most accurate predictor of future performance is past performance in similar situations. Behavioral interviewing, in fact, is said to be up to seven times more accurate than traditional interviewing, according to Schmidt and Conaway in their book *Results-Oriented Interviewing: Principles, Practices, and Procedures.*

Behavioral-based interviewing is touted as providing a more objective set of facts to make employment decisions than other interviewing methods. Traditional interview questions ask you general questions such as "Why should we hire you?" The process of behavioral interviewing is much more probing and works very differently.

In a traditional job interview, you can usually get away with telling the interviewer what he or she wants to hear, even if you are fudging a bit on the truth. Even if you are asked situational questions that start out "How would you handle XYZ situation?" you have minimal accountability. How does the interviewer know, after all, if you would really react in a given situation the way you say you would? In a behavioral interview, however, it's much more difficult to give responses that are untrue to your character. When you start to tell a behavioral story, the behavioral interviewer typically will pick it apart to try to get at the specific behavior(s). The interviewer will probe further for more depth or detail such as "What were you thinking at that point?" or "Tell me more about your meeting with that person," or "Who were the other people on the team?" or "Lead me through your decision process." If you've told a story that's anything but totally honest, your response will not hold up through the barrage of probing questions.

Employers use the behavioral interview technique to evaluate a candidate's experiences and behaviors so they can determine the applicant's potential for success. The interviewer identifies job-related experiences, behaviors, knowledge, skills, and abilities that the company has decided are desirable in a particular position and then structures very pointed questions to elicit detailed responses aimed at determining whether the candidate possesses the desired characteristics. Questions (often not even framed as a question) typically start out with "Tell about a time..." or "Describe a situation...." Clearly, these questions call for stories in response.

"Evidence shows that behavioral description questions require respondents to tell stories and that storytelling is now critical to applicants' success in employment interviews," write scholars Ralston, Kirkwood, and Burant, whose research in *Business Communication Quarterly* (2003) citing other academic studies of storytelling in behavioral interviewing. They suggest that stories told in interviews garner attention, serve as a way to make the applicant memorable, and describe past behavior in an appealing way.

Return to Alphabet Soup: Examples Using the Story Formulas

Career experts frequently advise job seekers to structure their stories based on the same formulas, expressed as acronyms, suggested in chapter 2 as overall structures for developing career stories. Following are stories told in each of the most common formats.

CAR: Challenge, Action, Result

> *Challenge:* In my last leadership role, we had a challenge with our receiving process. It would take five shipping-and-receiving associates about two days to process an average-sized shipment. I quickly recognized that with the holidays approaching, the size of our shipments would double, and our process had to change.
>
> *Action:* First, I addressed the overall stockroom organization and completely overhauled it. I collaborated with my stockroom manager to organize and label all products in every row. I directed rows to be organized by type of product. We were then able to sort boxes of product as they came off the trucks according to which row they went into. We had stockroom associates in each row and a runner who could carry boxes of product to their designated rows.
>
> *Result:* Receiving time was cut from two or three days to less than six hours from the time the truck hit the dock.

CCAR: Context, Challenge, Action, Result (developed by Kathryn Troutman)

Context: After Hurricane Katrina, our company was down for weeks.

Challenge: My subordinates are commissioned employees who still needed to collect a paycheck. Our print shop was up and running; however, the post office was not equipped to handle bulk mail, which is how our newspaper is distributed on Wednesdays. On weekends, our paper is distributed to stores. At this time we were doing neither.

Action: I suggested to the publisher that we distribute the paper to stores on Wednesdays. We all collaborated to come up with selling points for advertisers; for example, offering special discount to roofers, carpenters, and lawn-maintenance businesses for advertising in our services-offered section.

Result: Revenue started flowing again, and my team members got paid.

PAR: Problem, Action Result

Problem: My marketing plan for the admissions office of my college included placing some advertising in national print media, but we didn't have the financial resources to make that happen.

Action: I knew that one of our corporate partners wanted to promote its diversity initiatives. I proposed we develop a print advertising campaign cobranding the recruiting message.

Result: The final pieces delivered dual messages of recruitment for prospective students and recruitment/placement of potential diverse employees. Through this campaign, both messages were successfully received with increased admission interest and placement at the company. The project also launched more advertising initiatives at the school.

PARLA: Problem, Action, Result, Learning, Application (developed by Donald Asher)

Problem: During my Peace Corps experience as a volunteer in Guatemala, absolutely nothing ever went right. From no water and electricity for three weeks to getting to the health center on time by foot, donkey ride, and a canoe—to weighing a baby on a fish scale, hanging the scale from a thatched roof, and the roof coming down on me. Or putting on a conference in rural Guatemala and only one nurse shows up, and only briefly, too!

Action: I adjusted my attitude. I learned to adapt to conditions unlike anything I was accustomed to. I made up my mind to embrace the reality of life in Guatemala and the needs of those I served.

Result: Despite the frustrations, I began to make a difference in people's lives. For example, along with my team, I helped to ensure that more native children received inoculations against disease. The next time I put on a conference, I had learned enough about communicating with the local population to ensure better attendance.

Learning: I learned that expectations sometimes lead to disappointment and that I need to keep my expectations realistic. I bring that philosophy to all aspects of my life, especially blind dates, and live by the divine principle that everything happens for a reason, and 99 percent of the time, it is to learn a life lesson from it.

Application: Now, when I facilitate a meeting of professionals, and certain individuals show up and some do not, I don't get upset as much because the energy of those who attend enhances my facilitation and helps me learn.

SAR: Situation, Action, Result

Situation: Recently my firm was facing a huge turnover problem, especially in our technical staff because of lack of growth within the organization. No defined path was shared with the employees. To address the situation, I had not only a huge task of defining grades and identifying and compartmentalizing our employees' growth needs, but also a race against time.

Action: I knew the tasks would be time consuming, but I set a deadline for each piece. I aggressively collected information on the employee growth needs by sending questionnaires via e-mail and reaching out to the workforce. I compiled the data and determined short-term and long-term achievable goals. I developed a small-projects subset of the bigger project. I designed a system so that we could track each other's projects and meet every day. The most prominent finding was lack of challenge at work. I decided to implement a leadership program, effectively identifying the top 10 to 25 percent of workers suitable for the program based on performance reviews, peer reviews, and qualifications. I set an aggressive target of 15 days for each zone to complete this part of the survey.

Result: I met the deadlines, and by the end of the second month, we were ready with the budget for the training program, a targeted pilot training group, a location, and a trainer. We rolled out our first training on effective leadership, and by the end of the quarter, data showed that employees were now engaged and challenged. As a result, turnover was cut in half.

SCARQ: Situation, Challenge, Action, Result, Quantified (developed by Steve Gallison)

Situation: I had recently changed stores and become the new store's manager.

Challenge: The store had never engaged in community involvement or support and therefore had a rather tarnished image at the corporate level because the company is very committed to giving back to the community.

Action: I met with my staff and challenged them to come up with a relatively high-profile idea that would help the community. Under my leadership, the staff and I decided to raise money to buy high-tech fire helmets that would allow firefighters to see through the smoke.

Result: We met our fund-raising goal and earned a lot of positive press in the local community.

Quantified: The $10,000 we raised was more money than had ever been raised by any store in the chain.

SHARE: Situation, Hindrance, Action, Results, Evaluation (developed by Fred Coon)

Situation: A major bicycle corporation had been trying to collaborate with the state bicycling organization to create and establish a 25-unit bike-path signage program.

Hindrance: Because no one really knew how to get the program off the ground, it had been stalled for three years with no action.

Action: I joined the committee overseeing the project and immediately brought a fresh perspective to the group. I researched signs

I saw in another community and talked with manufacturers in the field. I ensured competitive pricing for the signs and suggested solutions for weather protection and anti-graffiti measures.

Results: The sign program was implemented just six months after I joined the committee.

Evaluation: I see these signs everywhere I go, and it gives me joy to see them. They bear testimony to my ability to execute a vision and get things done.

SIA: Situation, Impact, Analysis

Situation: Before I started in my most recent position, the city was paying a block premium rate to keep insurance companies in the black. When I came on board, I sought and demanded a full eligibility audit on enrollment figures.

Impact: This sole action generated immediate cost savings in the hundreds of thousands of dollars. I received public recognition for this action by the mayor and before the city council. I also discovered that other standard cost-containment strategies were never incorporated into benefit plans, which always made the city the primary carrier. I introduced a policy that eliminated this practice, which also positively impacted the city's benefit cost outlays.

Analysis: Having gotten these costs under control, I could focus on optimizing benefits packages for city employees.

SMART: Situation and More, Action, Results, Tie-In (developed by Susan Britton Whitcomb)

Situation and More: When I worked as a data-entry examiner in health-insurance claims, I was evaluated on two metrics, production and quality. My production was excellent; I keyed as much as 180 percent above expectations. However, my quality, as measured by keystroke error was always dipping below the 98.5 percent level of acceptance. I was not satisfied with that performance.

Action: I started to look for ways to work smarter. I learned to develop the habit of copying and pasting quickly. I developed macros and hot keys for repetitive keystrokes, and I trained myself to slow down when I started keying complicated information such as letter and number combinations.

Result: As a result of these improvements, my manager and I both observed a steady increase in my quality; I began to hit 100 percent every month.

Tie-in (which SMART originator Susan Britton Whitcomb describes as a theme or pattern that can link to key components the employer seeks, as well as communicate enthusiasm or job knowledge): This result set a pattern for my career in which I never had to settle for less than exceptional performance because I knew I could always find ways to improve.

SOAR: Situation, Obstacle, Action, Result

Situation: I once received a call from a patient who had a brain tumor for which he needed a very expensive and hard-to-get medication. In addition, he was having all sorts of insurance billing problems. He was literally driving from pharmacy to pharmacy looking to see which one had the medication in stock, but he had no luck.

Obstacle: I called a couple of pharmacies for him and was able to locate one; however, its satellite link went down, and the pharmacy refused to dispense the medication without successfully billing the patient's insurance company electronically. Normally we have nurses on call 24/7 for emergencies like this; however, I knew a company nurse would have told the patient to pay the several thousand dollars at the initial pharmacy I had found and seek reimbursement. There is no contingency for patients who didn't have the money.

Action: After a very exhaustive search, I located a specialty drug supplier that agreed to have the medication delivered by private carrier overnight. I gave the patient my personal cell number and asked him to call me if he did not receive his medication within 24 hours.

Result: A day later, I received a call from the patient's mother, thanking me for helping her son get the medication he needed for his brain tumor.

STAR: Situation, Task, Action, Result

Situation: Our company had just won a major outsourcing contract, resulting in spinning off 2,600 employees into a subsidiary within the parent organization.

Task: The company needed to develop an entire set of HR processes for this new subsidiary.

Action: I identified and developed all the processes, and then I created a resource intranet site containing powerful text and visuals illustrating the final version of all processes. I used the intranet site as the basis of a comprehensive training program for the spin-off company's HR team.

Result: The site became an ongoing reference tool to use long after the training. Having a documented process has been a valuable tool for the HR team. Corporate auditors can clearly see that we have defined and followed our processes.

The Classic Story Format

Another possible formula for telling stories in an interview is what scholars Sandra Morgan and Robert Dennehy describe as "the traditional framework of universal steps displayed in myths, hero stories, classic fairytales, ethnic stories, and many of your own family stories." The authors cite these "five sequential components" in a good story:

1. Setting
2. Build-up ("trouble's coming")
3. Crisis or climax
4. Learning
5. New behavior or awareness; in other words, "What did you learn?" and "How did you change?"

Example:

Setting: One of my customers wanted to get involved with digital printing, and since I knew our company had the technology and the capabilities, I set up a meeting to discuss this new technology.

Build-up: I pulled all the sales sheets from the intranet, gathered up samples, and prepared for my big opportunity. As I prepared, I made an initial call to the VP of sales for that particular business unit and let him know I had set this meeting to discuss the digital products.

Crisis or climax: What I did not know was that the customer was eager to proceed with this technology. The morning of the meeting, the customer had called in its own clients to lay out the project and launch date. As I walked into the meeting and the questions started, I knew I needed some help.

Learning: I explained to the group that I wanted to get the correct answers to these technical questions and would they mind if I brought in the VP of that division. After a few minutes, I was able to track down the VP, and we succeeded in pulling together the resources and staff to immediately start working on this project.

The reps from the client company were very impressed with the fact that I admitted I did not have all the answers and that I wanted to make sure they received the right information. I learned that it's best to be forthcoming and not try to fake my way through an important meeting or presentation.

New behavior or awareness: We are now producing monthly programs for this client using the digital print technology, and revenue for 2008 was $100,000 and projected at $200,000 for 2009. I've subsequently made it a point to anticipate contingencies better than I did in that situation—but also to know that I can bring in other resources when I have gaps in my knowledge.

Not Just Stories, but Stories Well Told

With storytelling well established as a way of responding to behavior-based questions, at least one scholarly study (by Ralston, Kirkwood, and Burant in 2003) focuses on how to measure and improve the quality of stories told in the interview. The authors present a set of criteria for an effective story to be used in a job interview:

- **Internal consistency:** Is the story cohesive? Does it avoid confusion and disjunction? Is the narrative consistent with the skills, abilities, and values the job seeker wants to portray?
- **Consistency with facts the listener knows to be true:** Does the story conform to what the interviewer is likely to have experienced or knows about the environment the job seeker is describing? Is it familiar and believable?
- **Relevance to question asked and claim being made:** In essence, does the story answer the question being asked? Does it provide appropriate evidence to support the skill, ability, knowledge, or characteristic the job seeker is claiming?
- **Univocality:** Is the story unambiguous? Does it lead to just a single conclusion or interpretation?
- **Detail that supports the claim being made:** Is the story revealing? Does it, in the words of Ralston, Kirkwood, and Burant, "provide telling details of plot, characterization, and action that enable listeners to see for themselves what the point is?"

- **Reflection of the job seeker's values, beliefs, sense of self/others, or emotional outlook:** Does the job seeker tell the story with sufficient passion so that it conveys a real sense of the applicant and how he or she might fit in with the employer's organization?

Interviewing expert Carole Martin adds that a frequent pitfall in telling effective interview stories is failing to provide sufficient details about the action portion of the story. The details enable you to paint a clear picture of the skill that facilitated the result. Martin recommends devoting 60 percent of a storied interview response to the action details and 20 percent each to the situation and result.

Storytelling for Traditional Interview Questions

While behavior-based responses are especially well suited to storytelling, you can tell stories in response to many other types of interview questions. One of these is the "question" that lends this book its title, "Tell me about yourself," which career writers Shelly Goldman and Wendy Enelow suggest is a great question to be asked because it "gives the candidate total control of the interview process" and is "a wonderful vehicle to build rapport."

A Personal Approach

Having interviewed 66 corporate human-resources executives, recruiters, hiring managers, and career experts for their book, *Insider's Guide to Finding a Job*, Goldman and Enelow learned that those who make hiring decisions often like to learn some personal information about candidates. Thus, in the sample responses to "Tell me about yourself" that follow, you'll find several instances of a more personal approach.

Much of who I am today was shaped by the fact that I come from a very big family in a small town. The number of Ellises in my town is more than 80, so I grew up constantly being compared to those who came before me. When I started playing football in high school, I heard constantly how good my cousins Brad and Lance were at football, and that helped me try just a little harder. In the classroom, it was my cousin Angie who set the standard for me to follow. Even within the last few years, as I have begun planting the seeds of a future public-service career, most introductions are quickly followed by "Are you one of THE Ellises?" Growing up in the shadow of my family wasn't bad, though. I had constant support in everything I ever tried, and because I am one of "THE Ellises," some doors have opened up for me that may not have opened otherwise. And because I constantly had to try to match the achievements of my forerunners, I worked hard and gained many rewards for my efforts. My family was on hand when I won a prestigious award for outstanding high school athlete for my achievements in football, track and field, weightlifting, and wrestling. When the door to my chosen college slammed in my face following the first of several knee surgeries, and my hometown university offered me a full academic scholarship, I jumped at the chance to shine in my own backyard. When I become the first Ellis to ever earn a college degree, I think you could hear the noise from miles away.

I am enthusiastic, creative, and extremely helpful, and I have had a lot of practice with problem solving. I have successfully completed many group projects, and working in groups is definitely something I love to do. I believe that work can be fun and challenging as well as serious. As a member of the American Marketing Association, I have shown that I am active in the marketing community. My job is also my hobby.

Many people and events throughout my life have shaped me into the person I am today. I have always greatly valued my family and friends because they have provided many opportunities for me; I am also fortunate to have had the chance to live in foreign countries, which has given me a new perspective on culture and people. Along the way, a significant stabilizer in my life has been classical music. Reading about the challenging lives of composers and musicians of the past and listening to the many emotionally profound and diverse pieces of music has turned me into a very patient, open-minded, curious, relaxed, and optimistic individual.

I was born and raised in India by a very loving and caring family. I moved to the United States five years ago and started high school a month later. Everything was new to me; the whole experience was shocking because of the cultural difference. The school, students, and the language were unfamiliar to me, and there were times when I really felt down and discouraged. In the first semester I had a tough time coming to terms with the whole new experience in school. But I did not give up; I asked for help when I needed it and worked hard. My experience has taught me to be resourceful and persistent.

I once wanted to be a film actor; however, as my aspirations progressed so did my career goals. Now I want to become a producer. I have realized my skills would be much better put to use as someone behind the scenes. I have a unique ability to understand people from diverse backgrounds and bring them together in a cohesive way so that things get done. This skill along with many others, I am convinced, will enable me to succeed in the entertainment industry.

Yes-or-No Questions

Yes-or-no questions also provide excellent opportunities for story-based responses. When employers ask yes-or-no questions, they don't expect one-word responses. They expect you to elaborate with examples that explain your yes-or-no response. Following are some examples:

Do you handle conflict well?

Yes. I am very passionate about human resources and see it as essential to an organization's success. Therefore, I often expect others to approach it with the same commitment and dedication that I do. Earlier in my career, I would sometimes come across as too black-and-white when trying to help keep department heads and administrators in legal compliance and regarding company policies. I've learned how important it is to understand the other person's perspective and tailor what you say so they can hear it. To help build this competency, I took a course on conflict management.

Are you a team player?

Absolutely. I once had a supervisor who did not have computer skills, but she was an excellent typist. Our computer system was very finicky and old, and the least quirk could render it inoperable. My typing skills were less than impressive, but I had better computer skills. More importantly, I could quickly learn these old computer programs, and I was sometimes able to fix problems with the computer. Between the two of us, we produced a newsletter, several reports, and fund-raising appeals. She had faith in me to deal with the computer and the patience to allow me to type at my own best speed, though she had no problem with contributing to the typing when we were under tight deadlines. In return I contributed my strong sales abilities in contacting contributors, which increased donations for our silent auction by 35 percent, which in turn increased our profits from a fund-raising event. She rewarded me with the chance to single-handedly organize a new fund-raiser in a smaller setting, and she acknowledged my efforts to the board members.

Do you handle pressure well?

Yes, and a good example came in the aftermath of Hurricane Rita when communications were virtually shut off. I had to respond appropriately to whatever problem arose and react very quickly without intervention from my supervisor or home-office support. I had to prioritize my own challenges and responses and come up with an action plan to fix whatever came along while conforming to company policy and procedures. It made me feel in control of the situation and fed my desire and ability to be a true leader.

Yes. My past experience as an administrative coordinator required me to deal with many serious situations since I held emergency on-call duties as a supervisor. One example was when I was called by a resident assistant to deal with an attempted suicide on her residence-hall floor. The situation required that I think clearly and quickly in this life-and-death situation. I had to weigh the many tasks that needed to be completed. I had to assign RAs to call 911, make sure the paramedics could get into the locked building, while at the same time applying first aid and ensuring that the rest of the residents on the floor were OK. I also had to make sure the privacy of the resident in need was respected. I basically prioritized and dealt with each task by its importance. I delegated responsibility to RAs for things that they were capable of handling because I could not physically be in many places at once. Once the resident was taken to the hospital, I handled the paperwork and followed up to make sure the staff members, residents, and the resident in need adjusted back to "normal" life. I know this is an extreme example not found in the financial consulting field; however, it shows just how well I can deal with tremendous pressure.

Would you describe yourself as goal-driven?

Yes, and I demonstrated my goal orientation as president of the local Jaycees, a community-service organization. I am very proud of the fact that I set a goal of signing 50 new members by the end of the year, and I accomplished that.

Absolutely. One of my recent goals as sales manager was to get an underperforming account executive who had been with the company for six months to start performing better and start nearing or exceeding goals. During his six-month performance evaluation, we confronted the numbers head-on and discussed ways to increase sales. I encouraged the employee's feedback and had him participate in generating ideas on how to boost sales, such as maximizing calls, managing his territory, and addressing his training needs. As a result, this salesperson hit his goals two of the last three months of the year and was close the third month. This was a big accomplishment for me as a manager because developing team members so they succeed is probably one of the most important goals a manager can have.

Other Traditional Questions

Stories, in fact, work well with most traditional interview questions, as in these examples.

How did you choose this career?

My father and I have always shared a love for music. When I was young, he took me to see a famous classical guitar player. Before this concert, I had always viewed classical music as something boring that only my grandparents listened to. To see the guitarist fuse together jazz and classical with such virtuosity brought the music to life in a way I had never experienced before. This performance alone inspired me to engage in music studies. I started as a performance major in college but decided to switch to marketing. I love performing, but I would much rather reach the masses by promoting music on a larger scale—in hopes that many young listeners can discover their love of music as I did.

I have been fascinated with the visual components of firms—logo designs, branding, signs, packaging—since I was very, very young. A speaker who designed logos for a living spoke to my fourth-grade class. I was a tiny artist with big aspirations, and I loved how a small image was used to convey so much information.

I was introduced to marketing and entrepreneurship through my high school club called DECA. I became vice president and participated in multiple national competitions, which contributed to my marketing knowledge. My college sales job gave me first-hand experience in relationship marketing and implementing a strategic plan to improve business throughout 15 Miami suburbs. From then on, I've devoted myself to understanding marketing and gaining knowledge on how to better apply new techniques to specific industries.

I knew I wanted to be a photographer since the first time I held my father's camera. I was about eight years old, and the camera was bigger than I was. He taught me how to use it, and we went out and took pictures of my horses. Later, we went to his darkroom and developed the pictures. After seeing the results, I knew that this was what I wanted to do with my life.

I knew that I wanted to pursue information systems technology about my sophomore year in college. It was then that I realized that my hobby, computers, was taking up most of my time. My favorite courses were IT courses. I also realized when I was doing computer-oriented work-study that I enjoyed it so much that I would have done it for free.

What accomplishment are you most proud of?

I was sent to one of our branch banks that was notorious for not growing its loan base. The branch had logged $75,000 in new loans in an 18-month period prior to my arrival. Having a reputation as a "hired gun" when it came to loan production, I succeeded in soliciting and booking $700,000 in my first six months at the branch.

I have been lucky enough in my life to have positive role models, so it has been a goal of mine for a long time to create a safe haven for young women ages 13–16 to empower and encourage them to be critical thinkers, to have a positive self-image, and to prepare for their bright futures. I have found a way to organize annual retreats and various events and seminars throughout the year by incorporating all of the organizations that I'm involved with. This effort started out as a program that I chaired for my sorority, but because of limited funds, we got to put on only one retreat, which was not enough to accomplish my goal. Last year I began to revisit my plan. I created a committee of five of my sorority sisters in different cities who are involved with various organizations. Each one agreed to recruit five girls to attend the retreat. We've held the first retreat, which was a huge success.

Last semester my university's Council for Student Activities selected me for its team. The group negotiates contracts of entertainers, sets up sound equipment, markets the entertainers to students, and generally decides what kind of programming should be presented. When I was hired, I didn't know the first thing about how to fill any of those responsibilities. I decided, however, that I wasn't going to fail. Four months later, I have become the Webmaster for the group. I also write our campus newsletter and created Game Night, a student competition of table games. That event yielded the biggest audience ever for a non-concert event.

Tell me about a mistake you've made.

My TV station where I was an associate producer planned to run a story about a case of hepatitis that was contracted through a local restaurant. The reporter had been sent out late for the story, and he was very late in gathering information. By the time he had his piece together, it was nearly time for it to air. I had to hurry just to get his subtitles on the air, and as I talked to him on the phone, I didn't have time to listen to what he was planning to say live. He yelled something to me right before he hung up, and I said OK, even though I didn't know what he planned to say.

When we got on the air, he told viewers that if they thought they had hepatitis, they should call 911. I took responsibility for his mistake. I learned that when a story is that important, you can't take chances. The story needed to be moved or cut off to be aired correctly.

Why should we hire you?

The evolution of my career demonstrates that I can make an immediate and positive contribution in this position. Through hard work and diligence, my professional career has been a bit of a rags-to-riches story. When I first started working full-time after college, I took an entry-level job as a file clerk at a major insurance company. From the beginning, I was motivated to be much more. I worked my way up through the ranks into the positions of claims data-entry operator, claims examiner, and then underwriter. When I left this company, I went on to become a retirement plan administrator, then onto benefits specialist. Ultimately, I became an assistant finance director in charge of group benefits and workers' comp for the City of Scarsdale. My progressive learning process was not based on theory picked up in a classroom; I gained knowledge through actually researching and performing essential job-related functions. Primarily, I am a fast learner, and if hired, I intend to minimize your training and hiring costs, because I have always been motivated to learn, even if it means personally investing my time and resources as part of the process.

My abilities in so many areas—sales, marketing, promotions, and management—will be invaluable for your company, including my experience working with people with diverse backgrounds and at different levels, my background working with various clients, my work overseeing sales teams, my eye for detail, and the fact that I strive to do the best job possible at all times. I'm also reliable, loyal, and trustworthy...and if you hire me, you will have a team player who will add to the integrity and quality of your sales force for years to come. As an example of the kind of results I get that would justify your hiring me: Sales were down in the electronics department of the retail store at which I worked as an assistant manager. The perception was that our products were inferior to a competitor. I took the initiative to create excitement at the store level to increase sales. I attained buy-in from my manager so that I could run a contest. I collected sales data from the store on our products and used that information to back the need for this contest. My manager loved the idea. He thought it was exciting and loved the fact that I provided him with details on how I planned to track the sales process. In the end, I increased sales for that month by 100 percent, which was phenomenal.

What personal weakness has caused you the greatest difficulty in school or on the job?

My greatest weakness had been delegation. I used to take it upon myself to do many small projects throughout my shift as a manager that could have been done by others. Once I realized that I was doing more work than the other assistant managers, and they were achieving better results, I reevaluated what I was doing. I quickly realized that if I assign each person just one small project at the beginning of their shift, clearly state expectations for the project, and then follow up, everything will get done, and I can manage much more efficiently and actually accomplish much more.

More Examples: Typical Questions and Storytelling Answers

This section contains typical interview questions, both behavioral and traditional, and sample story-based responses to them. Note that many of these stories contain emotional content to draw the interviewer in and help him or her identify with the interviewee.

Persistence, Goal-Setting, Commitment, Initiative

Give me an example of how you've demonstrated persistence.

I volunteer for Big Brothers/Big Sisters. I was very eager to meet my first "little sister," but nothing prepared me for what I would be up against. Libby was a 10-year-old second grader whom I had to teach to read. When I met her, she seemed very nice, but she turned out to be one tough customer. Libby really didn't like to read and would try any way possible to avoid it. During our first couple of meetings, I let her pick out the books that we would read. I didn't notice that Libby was fooling me. It took until the third week of our meetings for me to finally notice that she had memorized the books that we were "reading." I was shocked but quickly decided that I would pick out the books during our meetings. Week after week, I would visit her, and she would think up a way to get out of reading. During our hour-long meetings, we would read and play a game. I was determined to help her learn how to read, no matter what this crafty second grader could think up. It took weeks of long games, finding deeply buried toys in the playground sand, and searches for her "missing" book bag before she gave up. Finally, we picked up the books again, just as we had all those weeks before. This time when she scanned the pages, she was amazed to find that she could read.

I was 14 when I first started to work as a trail guide and trainer at a ranch. I have loved horses my entire life and could not have imagined a better job. When I first started working at the ranch, I had basic riding skills and training techniques, but every day I would put 100 percent into learning how to become a better rider and trainer. At 16, I had been working at the ranch for two summers and was given my first horse to personally train. Training a horse can be extremely difficult and potentially a very dangerous process. This big, beautiful two-year-old quarter horse was all my responsibility. Every day I worked with her, starting by teaching her to walk, stop, go, and turn on a lead line. This process was grueling because it takes time and a lot of patience. After a few weeks of ground training, she seemed ready for a saddle and rider, but she would buck, spin, and jump to try and throw me off. Day in and day out I worked with her, and every time I would get bucked off, I would pick myself up, no matter how hard it hurt, and get back on her. She taught me persistence and patience, and I learned a lot more about myself through this experience. It took three months for her to become a perfectly behaved, wonderful riding horse. I had bruises, scars, and near-death experiences, but this experience has changed my life forever. What I learned in training this horse has carried on into every aspect of my life.

Describe a time when you stood your ground for a principle you believed in.

When I was a bureau chief and reporter, my editor wanted an in-depth interview with the family of a young girl who'd fallen through the ice at a nearby lake and was in a coma with brain damage. We clashed on the morality and sensitivity of doing such a story for the sake of headlines, and I ultimately convinced the editor that shining a spotlight on a family so obviously grief-stricken was not a good course of action. We held the stories until after the girl recovered and was no longer in critical condition.

Describe a project or idea that was implemented or carried out successfully primarily because of your efforts.

I had been recently selected as the head swim team coach for the YMCA I was employed with. A swim meet was just around the corner, but only five swimmers had enrolled for the program, none of whom had ever been a part of an organized team. Funding would be cut for the team if more interest could not be generated. So I decided that I would take action and actively recruit people to join. Not only did I have to run the practices and correct any technical mistakes the swimmers were making, but I also had to contact other local swim teams to invite them to join the meet. I had to meet with the parents and the children separately and organize a way to help pay for t-shirts, swimsuits, goggles, and swim caps. By the third week of the program, I had gained 15 more swimmers, and every single one had beat his or her own time in practice. When the meet came, I organized the events, ordered ribbons, and recruited volunteers. At the end of the meet, my team had come in first place among four other teams. The parents were delighted, and the profits from the swim team had skyrocketed, to the approval of the board of directors.

Give me an example of a time when you set a goal for yourself and successfully pursued it.

I feel very strongly that an orientation program is critical to employee success and the success of an organization. My goal was to implement an effective program across the company. I recognize that some goals can take time, so I have implemented the program over several years. The first step was to design an orientation session with the regional vice president. The second step was designing and implementing orientation protocols for each employee group for supervisors' use, which have been very positively received by department administrators. The third step was designing a six-week orientation program for administration staff and modeling this program company-wide. This program has earned very positive feedback and ensures that supervisors provide a detailed orientation and that opportunities to connect with key constituencies are provided early on. I refined the orientation sessions, and I combined supervisor and staff orientations—which oriented employees to the company's history, mission, values, and services—in 2008 for the most successful and well-attended session yet. The program has also fostered interdisciplinary, interdepartmental connections.

I had a long-term goal to become an excellent program manager. I applied myself in developmental positions and learned the ins and outs of the organization from the bottom up. I got to know the staff and managers well. I volunteered for projects to enhance and streamline the existing workflow. In doing so, I had an opportunity to apply for a temporary management position and obtained it. Through four years in this acting position, I strived to continuously learn and improve processes and policies. I have brought forward many success stories that have been recognized by the corporation and have earned several awards for these achievements.

My first few years in banking had me on the fast track to branch management. I realized at some point along the way that my true passion was in offering financial advice not limited to checking accounts and loans. It was at that point that I made arrangements to go back to school full-time to pursue my goal, which I am just about to achieve.

Attending my college has been a dream of mine since I was seven years old. Twenty years later, after a few detours, I completed my Associate of Arts degree and applied to my university as a transfer student. I will never forget the call I received from Ginger in the admissions office telling me that I had been accepted! I was elated! But there was one problem. My husband is an active-duty soldier, and I had to somehow convince the U.S. Army to move us from our current duty station to somewhere closer to my school—not an easy task. My husband requested to be placed on special duty as a recruiter and subsequently was, but we still had to get placed near my school. First, I spoke with a sergeant who was a recruiter near the school. He said he could assist us in getting stationed in the area, but I soon learned he had no control over where people were placed. But I didn't let that roadblock stop me. I then wrote a letter to the sergeant in charge of regional recruiting to request his assistance. After a week of no response, I sent a letter to the general in charge of ALL recruiting. I then contacted my congressman to request that he write a letter to the army on my behalf. The congressman was happy to help. About a week later, the congressman called to tell me that my letters had made their way to the Pentagon and to call Ginger and let her know I would be attending school in the fall! I was thrilled!

The summer before my senior year of college, I moved to the Mississippi Gulf Coast to live with my aunt and uncle. I wanted to get away from my annual routine, experience a new place, and make some money. My uncle is a general contractor and builds high-end custom homes for various people in the Gulf area. That summer I was employed as a general laborer, and it was the hardest physical work I have ever endured for the lowest amount of pay I have ever earned. I met some rough men and had to deal with a daily barrage of insults and derogatory language. However, I worked through the 104-degree days in 90 percent humidity. It was a learning experience. Although the work was hard and the company was unpleasant, I learned a lot. I learned to work hard, but to look at the bigger picture. I never thought about quitting and going home, although it was always an option. I stuck it out, made some friends, and made some money. I had made a goal and made it happen. My summer in Mississippi made me better.

Problem-Solving

Tell me about a time you came up with an innovative solution to a problem.

During the Y2K project I led in 1999, our area had a power outage at approximately 10:40 p.m. New Year's Eve that threatened to shut down our systems at the midnight hour—which was abjectly critical for Y2K. I instructed our lead technician to pull the battery backups from the cafeteria refrigerators for use in our server room, which at the time did not have an individual backup power system. The power outage lasted until nearly 3 a.m., but our use of the battery backups saved 100 percent of our rolled data. Although using the backups caused all dairy products in the refrigerators to spoil, the cost of restocking the dairy products was later determined to be less than 2 percent of the projected customer data loss to the business had we not used my solution.

The trucks at the retail store at which I worked as an assistant manager came loaded by personnel at a distribution center, box by box. After receiving a few trucks, I noticed that my employees were unloading broken merchandise that took a lot of time to clean up before the rest of the truck could be finished. The broken glass, paint, or whatever material it was prevented the employees from proceeding farther into the truck, causing more person-hours than normal. I noticed that the merchandise was broken because heavier boxes were on top of lighter boxes. After a couple of days of this situation, with productivity decreasing, I learned that the rest of the stores in my district faced the same problem. As a result, I asked each store to take pictures of the mess so the distribution centers could see exactly what was happening. I also asked each one to write down how many additional person-hours it took to clean up the mess. After we gathered this information for a four-week period, we had a pretty a good estimate of how much the company was losing—approximately $9.50 per person-hour, an average of $125 per store times 15 stores times 30 nights a month, amounting to a substantial sum. I took the information to my district manager. Once he realized how much money his district was losing each month because of broken merchandise in the trucks, he contacted his regional manager, and the trucks after that were loaded more carefully. The district made our Profit and Loss the next month by a 9 percent increase.

My older brother is deaf. Growing up, his deafness made our relationship very challenging and complicated. It goes without saying that siblings should be able to communicate on a certain level. During my childhood I had to overcome obstacles that other kids didn't. In addition to emotional struggles of coping with having a deaf brother, I had to find a new form of communication to break this language barrier. While the rest of my family used a new form of deaf communication called cued speech, my brother and I solely communicated by reading each other's lips and talking with no voice. While I was given obvious options for how to solve the communication problem, I decided to choose something completely different and unique, something that my brother to this day still appreciates and finds exciting. Not only has this approach brought my brother and me closer, the experience and the way my brother and I now interact has shown how I overcame this adversity and broke the social norms of the deaf community. My brother is a very independent and driven person; however, to this day I have been able to sustain good communication with him.

When I hosted a radio talk show, I prepared material for an interview with a state senate candidate only to find out when he arrived that he would not discuss any issues in my prepared material. I literally had to conduct an hour-long one-on-one interview using only the knowledge I had off the top of my head. Knowing I couldn't carry an entire show with little material to work from, I broke format 10 minutes into the broadcast and turned the show into a live call-in and built upon questions from those posed by listeners. The subject, who went on to become a state senator, thoroughly enjoyed the hour, gave me special considerations for coverage later in the campaign, and granted me primary access for his first in-seat interview.

Give me a specific example of a time when you used good judgment and logic in solving a problem.

I had a client come into the bank where I worked and request a $5,000 personal loan to "pay off some bills." In the customary review process, I determined that what was really needed was a $25,000 debt-consolidation loan. Rather than giving the customer a "quick-fix" to the problem, I logically solved the problem in a way that was in the best interest of both the bank and the client.

What steps do you follow to study a problem before making a decision?

Following standard models for problem-solving and decision-making can be very helpful. Here are the steps and how they helped me solve a problem with a group project:

1. ***Define the problem to be solved and decision to be made.*** *For a project in an introductory management class, the assignment was to report on the corporate structure and financial situation of a couple of companies. The decision to be made was what companies to profile and how to present the information.*
2. ***Gather the necessary information.*** *Some group members wanted to report on automakers while others wanted to do electronics firms. We gathered information on both types of companies.*
3. ***List all possible choices.*** *We made lists of companies in both categories.*
4. ***Consider possible outcomes for each choice.*** *We decided that a report about car companies could have a positive outcome, but one about electronics firms might be more futuristic with high-tech products such as nanotechnology computers, hologram technologies, and digital home theaters.*
5. ***Check out how you feel about each of the choices.*** *Given that this was a group project, we had to consider the feelings of all group members.*
6. ***Relate the choices to your values and priorities.*** *Again, all group members weighed in on their values and priorities.*

7. ***From the possible alternatives, choose one.*** *We decided that we'd do electronics companies because we could bring in products from each company and show what lies ahead.*

8. ***Commit yourself to your chosen decision and disregard the others. Concentrate your energies in one direction.*** *Once we made our decision, we focused all our work on electronics firms.*

9. ***Take steps to turn your decision into positive action.*** *All group members got interested in how the companies were doing.*

10. ***Evaluate your progress from time to time. Change your decision if necessary.*** *We were pleased with our progress and didn't feel a need to change our decision. We got an A on the project.*

We can sometimes identify a small problem and fix it before it becomes a major problem. Give an example of how you have done this.

When I worked in a large retail store, the standard procedure was to leave a product on the shelf until the supply ran out, and then place more items out. This practice obviously wasted a lot of person-hours. Of interest particularly to me were the air conditioners. Not only did I have to put the heavy things on the shelves, but also they were selling at a very high rate. So if somehow AC units ran out on a day in which I could not restock them, they would not be available to customers. As a result I started making a list of products, including the AC units, that the overnight stock people could put on the shelves. As a result, the people on duty always had a job to do, so labor hours were not wasted, and the shelves were always stocked full of product.

Describe a specific problem you solved for your employer.

When I was working as a receptionist at an apartment complex, a tenant argued that he had turned in his rent payment the day it was due. He stated that he had slipped it under the door because our office was closed for the day. I decided to consult my manager because I realized that maybe the office needed a sign that stated that we did not accept rent money that is slipped under the door. My boss agreed, and we posted the sign. We never again had a problem with tenants who claimed they'd paid their rent that way.

Have you found any ways to make your job easier or more rewarding or to make yourself more effective?

I find that taking a proactive mindset to recognizing and solving problems before they happen make any job more rewarding. It not only saves time and effort, but also gives me a sense of accomplishment and ownership in my job. I demonstrated my proactive approach when I worked at a major supermarket chain. As a bookkeeper, I oversaw the offices. The safe was kept outside of the office in front of the cash registers, where anyone could get inside it if I or another office associate had it open to drop a deposit or get money in and out. I realized that the situation was a security hazard. Although we could not move the safe to the inside of the office where it was more secure, I ordered a timelock compartment and had it installed so the safe could be opened only at a specific time when the store closed each day. Money could be dropped through a slot in the compartment door, and we kept large sums of money in that compartment. We kept operating cash on hand since we needed some excess money to perform daily functions. One month after I left that store, I learned that it was robbed. Because of my efforts and foresight, the robbers got only a small amount of cash. My previous supervisor thanked me for my efforts, which gave me a great feeling, and I carried this proactive mindset to my other jobs thereafter.

Persuasive Communication and Presentations

Tell me about a time you had to sell or persuade someone on an idea of yours.

The business team had a very tight deadline for getting FDA approval for a line extension of a newly marketed pharmaceutical product. The team wanted to do something very quickly, focusing only on efficacy and safety and not including any outcomes. I convinced the team to include some outcomes related to convenience, satisfaction, and sleep quality. I had to convince them that this information was critical for us to gain market access, especially related to managed-care formularies. The FDA approved the line extension.

Annually, a year-end tournament capped off lessons at my tennis club. However, students had started losing interest in the tournament. Three years ago, I figured out a way to motivate the kids to play in the tournament by making it much more age-friendly. I suggested to the head coach that we all pitch in to buy prizes for the students and trophies for the winners and have other games and exercises going on while the tournament took place. The result was a 40 percent increase in participants and a significant increase in the crowds of family and friends that came out to watch.

In one of my marketing classes, we had to read case studies of problematic business scenarios, evaluate them, and tell what changes we would make in the way the company was managed. The cases were very confusing, and students had a hard time separating issues. I went to my professor to suggest role-playing the characters in the cases and proceed as if it were real life—to give students a better understanding. At first she snubbed my idea and thought that students would not take it seriously. However, I was very persistent. I told her that since I am a very visual learner and knew that it would help me, I therefore felt the approach could make a difference in the class. She still refused. I then asked her to give me just one case to try my idea. I said that I would take one of the roles and a volunteer could take another. I said that if the idea failed, I would never mention it again. She gave me my chance, and it worked! My idea grabbed the attention of the class. Instead of reading the boring cases and going around the room sharing our thoughts, I got the class involved and excited about the material that we were learning.

As an account executive, I persuade potential advertisers all the time. But I specifically remember persuading the owner of a tanning salon to advertise in the middle of the winter after he had already declined at the beginning. I used my personal experience as a sorority member to explain to him that winter is the best time to advertise tanning salons because sororities have formals, and members want to look tan in their dresses. He knew sororities were a huge part of his business and agreed to advertise for the rest of the school year as long as I kept him up to date on good times to run specials for sororities.

I was the leader of my macroeconomics group in college. As leader, I had to delegate parts of the assignment to other group members. Not only did I do a written section for each paper, but I also gathered all of the props we needed for our oral presentation, and I typed all of the five papers assigned. I was also taking four other classes at the time. By the fourth paper, I decided to persuade some of the other group members to edit and finalize it. I learned a lot about delegation and leadership when I discovered that they were happy to help out.

Describe a situation in which you were able to use persuasion to successfully convince someone to see things your way.

Recently my company asked for bids on a phone system for our new training center. Two companies came in very close with their bids, and most of my department wanted to go with a vendor that we have used in the past. After I looked over the proposals, it was clear that this was the wrong decision. So, I talked individually with each member of our staff and changed their minds. We got the best product, saved money, and provided the highest quality.

Describe the most significant or creative presentation that you have had to complete.

The most significant presentation I have ever had to deliver was at a national research symposium. I was presenting research I had completed on digital analysis of mammograms and had to present to a panel of more than 100 judges who were at the top of their field. I focused on the research, which could sell itself, and just let the information flow. It went over very well, and I received many more invitations to present the research, including on national television.

I have grown to be a confident presenter. My most successful presentation took place in my current job when I was asked to present a leadership-development program for a class of management trainees. The point of my program was to teach each trainee his or her leadership style, so he/she knew how to interact on his or her floor as a student leader. The most significant aspect of this program is that it taught them about their leadership styles without their knowing it. Each trainee filled out a general questionnaire that asked about preferences. Each person, according to his or her responses, was assigned to a group. I then gave each group a book to read. Each group had to read a portion aloud, after which I explained how each group tackled the task. They all had handled the task differently. Each trainee successfully understood how he or she approached tasks, and from that how they would approach their job as managers. Not only did I engage the audience in what was being presented, I have since seen the program adapted in other presentations by trainees in that class. Not only did they enjoy it, they learned something about themselves that would help them help their subordinates.

Give me a specific example of a time when you sold your supervisor or professor on an idea or concept.

Last summer, I wanted to help organize a summer camp for local low-income children. My supervisor knew the demand would be there but feared we would not have enough staff. I convinced her that because I went to the facility daily, I could network with acquaintances and convince them of the importance of this camp. My supervisor trusted me. We had hundreds of children sign up for the program, and I had reached so many people that we were able fully staff the camp as well as have a backup supply of people who were willing to volunteer their time and services to the organization.

Flexibility, Adaptability, Taking Responsibility

Give me an example of a time you had to rise to the occasion and take on new responsibilities.

Two summers ago my father, who was the backbone of my family, had a massive stroke and was left partially paralyzed. This happened just a few short months before I was supposed to start attending college, and at the time I didn't know if I ever would go to school. My dad put me in charge of his online business, which I had known very little about. I turned into the sole provider for my family overnight. I spent my days on the computer by my father's hospital bed, very thankful that I could work and still stay by his side. My father kept getting better and better and eventually went back to work for himself. In a very short time, I realized that taking care of your family is the most important thing you can do, and to do so, you need to work hard and succeed so that you can provide them with everything they need.

Tell me about a time you went above and beyond to get a job done.

We had to lay people off a couple years ago, and the vice president asked me for my recommendations while I was out on vacation. Because I had been meeting regularly with the directors and had been leading a workforce planning effort, I had very clear data from them regarding those areas where reductions could be made with the least disruptions to key services. I took the time during my vacation to share that data with the VP. The result was that the decisions were made in a timely way and the impact on services was minimal.

Although I had already punched out, I stayed behind to help a colleague solve a problem. A customer was very angry, as he had waited a long time for his coffee. My colleague was new, and she was quite slow. I came out and explained things to the customer. Although he was very angry at first, I just listened to him and told him that we try to bring our best out to each customer who walks into our store. After a discussion, he left with a happy face and was satisfied.

While working at a large retailer, I was one of three people to work in the electronics department. One day upon arriving at work, I was told the district manager was coming the next day to do a store inspection. The two other people who worked in electronics were both over 55. Neither could lift heavy objects, and one refused to work at all. As a result, the electronics department was usually left to me to keep in order and stocked with product. I had about five hours of work time to get the entire department in order. After the five hours passed, there was still a substantial amount of work to be done. I asked the store manager if I could stay and work after hours while the overnight stockers were there. He said that because of the employment budget, he could not let me. So I was faced with bringing the entire store's rating down or not getting paid. I worked without pay, and three hours later, the department was in tip-top shape. The electronics department got a score of 95 out of 100.

I don't believe in trying to get by with the least possible effort, and I am always willing to go beyond the call of duty to perform an assignment successfully. My anthropology class was given a group project in which each group had to teach a topic to the class for 50 minutes. I was a freshman and everyone in my group was either juniors or seniors, so I was very nervous and felt that I needed to prove myself. My topic was Botswana. I went online for hours, as well as to the library trying to find as much info as possible, but there just wasn't enough to fill a 50-minute presentation. Instead of working with the little material that I had, I continued to search in other libraries. I ended up writing a very good paper. In addition, I taught myself how to use PowerPoint, and came up with a substantial slide show. I met with my group, and they were amazed at the work I had done. My team earned an A for the project.

By providing examples, convince me that you can adapt to a wide variety of people, situations, and environments.

I've shown my ability to adapt by successfully working in several very different jobs. For example, I lived with a native family in Costa Rica. I worked as a nanny for a famous writer in Cape Cod. I was responsible for dealing with Drug

Court participants. And I catered to elite country-club clientele. I did it all well and had no trouble adapting.

Give an example of how you applied knowledge from previous coursework to a project in another class.

Last semester I was taking a microeconomics course and a statistics course. One of the microeconomics projects dealt with showing the relationship between the probability that customers would stop buying a product if the price was raised a certain amount. Through what I learned in statistics, I could find the median where the price was the highest and still kept most of the customers happy.

Handling Difficult Situations

Tell me about a time when you made the best of a negative situation.

During my first spring break as a college student, I was helping one of my friends from high school move to a new place. While I was there for the weekend, I did something that was extremely irresponsible. I received a ticket for racing. I had never before gotten into any major trouble. My drive home to tell my parents what I had done was the longest drive I have ever had to make. After explaining to them what happened and being ordered to perform 250 hours of community service by the court, I felt like burying myself. I did not want to see the light of day. However, instead of feeling down and out, I was determined to repay my debt to the community and rebuild my reputation. For the entire summer, I worked outside in the heat throwing away furniture and odds and ends at a thrift store for six to seven hours a day, six days a week. I not only repaid my debt, but I also lost 45 pounds while working in the heat and working out at the YMCA every day during the summer. Thanks to this experience, I improved myself mentally and physically.

When I was in the third grade my mother decided to start up her own restaurant and bar. The business took up a lot of her time. She would go into work at 8 a.m. and then come home around 2 a.m. the next morning. When my father was transferred to another city, my mother decided to stay behind and take care of the business. The only way my brother and I got to see at least one parent for a significant amount of time was go to the restaurant for periods of time during the day. The business became our second home. Some nights we would sleep in the office until 2 a.m., and some days we would sit in the office all day and help our mother with office work. Some days one of her waitresses, cooks, or bus boys would pick us up from school, and we'd and go stay with our mother for a couple of hours and then be sent home when the dinner rush came. We would go to the bar on Saturday mornings at 9 a.m. after a busy Friday night and help the cleaning crew sweep the beer-soaked peanut shells off the floor. I never thought it was weird or wrong that we spent so much of young lives in a bar. It was a place to see my mother. I learned things about the restaurant business that not many other children get to learn at such an early age. Not even some adults have learned as much as I have about the restaurant business. I watched and learned from my mother, and I feel today that those years of observation have made me who I am in the workplace. I learned that you have to be nice to people. Even though I rarely saw either of my parents for three years, that absence has forced me to realize that you are not always going to have mommy and daddy take care of you, and eventually you have to be self-sufficient and not depend on anyone because they are not always going to be there.

I was in my 10th-grade year in high school when I began getting into a lot of trouble both at home and at school. I was becoming a disruption in my classes, and my grades began to fall dramatically. My parents were worried about me, and so was I. I didn't know what I wanted to do in life. With about three weeks left to go in the year, I was expelled from school. I was sent to an "alternative school," which did not provide any classes to actually further my education, so I stopped going. My parents began to home-school me, and during the summer of my 10th-grade year, I began taking college classes. I realized that high school was not for me, and at the beginning of the next year, I enrolled full-time in community college. I learned at this point that it takes hard work, dedication, and determination to succeed. Over the next year and a half, I earned my associate's degree at just 17. From there I transferred to a four-year university, where the same values paid off.

Tell me about a situation that tested your coping skills.

Two years ago, my brother committed suicide. I am a call-center representative, and people call with all sorts of problems that seemed very trivial to me in the state of mind I was in after my brother's death. It was very hard to separate my pain and sadness from my professional life. I would mentally prep myself each day knowing that the people I was talking to did not know what happened. I had to detach myself so I could provide excellent customer service. I sought out special projects to complete for my manager until I was ready to return to the high pressures of my demanding job.

Arriving at the language school I was attending in Costa Rica in the middle of the night with minimal Spanish-language skills, I found my way to a very small town with no street addresses or names and found my temporary residence. I was scared, but I handled the situation well, very calmly. In stressful situations, I am always the one in the group to stay calm and focused. My friends, family, and professors have always said that I am an oasis of calm in a storm.

Describe an instance when you had to think on your feet to extricate yourself from a difficult situation.

When I was a resident assistant at my college, a student I did not know asked me if he could use my phone to call another room. Although I did not know the student, I allowed him into my room. He used the phone and in the course of his conversation, he stated that he had just come from a fraternity party and was high from taking some drugs. After this conversation, I had to enforce the student conduct code by writing him up. He became very hostile toward me and would not give me any identification or information. I stood in the doorway to prevent him from leaving. I noted the serial numbers on his keys, so when the situation got to the point where I felt unsafe, I allowed him to leave. I still performed my job without jeopardizing my or his physical welfare.

Sometimes it's easy to get in over your head. Describe a situation where you had to request help or assistance on a project or assignment.

It's impossible to know everything in the IT field because of rapidly changing technology, so recently when we were having troubles with our circuit emulation over our ATM network, I had to call in some engineers from North Carolina to come help me out. The nice thing about asking for help is that when you get the assistance, you can learn from what you are told and apply it to future situations.

Recall a time from your work experience when your manager or supervisor was unavailable and a problem arose.

My supervisor was absent once when I was in charge of a soccer game. An actual assault took place at the game. A player hit the referee. With no supervisor to turn to, I immediately called the police, who quickly restored order to the situation. I felt I made an effective decision.

Describe a time when you were not very satisfied or pleased with your performance. What did you do about it?

I failed my first business calculus test, which made me very unhappy. I wasn't going to let this incident set the trend for the rest of the semester. I went to my counselor and arranged to meet with a tutor once a week. My tutor helped me out incredibly. My grades soon improved, and I went on to redeem myself from my one slip-up on the first test.

Describe a situation in which you found that your results were not up to your supervisor's expectations.

Recently, I was asked to put together a proposal for a migration of network systems. Misunderstanding my boss, I thought it was just an informal paper. When I presented it to him days later, he was upset with the quality since it had to be presented to our VP. I explained my misunderstanding, apologized, reworked the paper, and had it back to him with enough time for him to review it before he presented it successfully at the meeting.

Tell me about a difficult situation when it was desirable for you to keep a positive attitude. What did you do?

While directing a play, I was faced with numerous problems. The sets were not coming together; the performers were fighting and not working hard; the technical aspects of the play were far from complete; and in general it was a mess. I was also the stage manager, which means that I tell people when to go on stage and tell the crew when to bring pieces of the set on stage. So I organized everything and told people to do specific jobs and asked them in a firm yet positive manner. People began to have fun, and the production went on extremely well. All performances sold out. The play was regarded as one of the smoothest shows produced by the group.

Management, Leadership

How have you used communication skills to manage employees?

I inherited a long-term poor-performing sales rep who would not follow through on the plan of action we discussed during our field ride-along. He was also a poor listener who would always try to turn situations around and blame others for his failures. I found that communicating with him in writing left the ball in his court, and he could refer back to my written communications when needed. Putting things in writing also left a paper trail to show the rep's progress. The experience taught me that you have to treat each rep individually and find out the best way to communicate with him or her.

I had a very difficult employee who constantly challenged my authority. I took the time to understand this employee in meetings, as well as by gathering information from clients and coworkers. I conducted regular meetings with her and brought to her attention some of her greatest strengths and my expectations. I opened the lines of communication with this employee and found that her greatest strength was to help people. I accepted her for her uniqueness and constantly praised her for her great accomplishments. I brought to her attention areas she needed to improve. In the end, it's a great success story. She has earned my trust, and I trust her ability to represent the organization in a very professional manner. She now takes the lead in team meetings and helps others see their full potential. She is now one of our best team players.

In a supervisory or group leader role, have you ever had to discipline or counsel an employee or group member?

As president of a community-service organization, I was faced with a board member not carrying out his duties as management development vice president. I consulted with him as to what we could do together to fix the problem. We agreed that he really couldn't devote the time that it took to carry out certain projects, and he ended up resigning his position, but he also stated he would help his replacement in whatever capacity he could. It made me feel as though we had come to the conclusion together rather than the VP thinking I was criticizing his performance, which was not the case. I had a plan of action and carried it out successfully.

Interpersonal Communication, Teamwork, Team Leadership

Can you give me an example of your team-leadership skills?

Designing the staffing plan for my company is an excellent example of my team-leadership skills. I needed the input of corporate leadership and front-line employees to design a model aligned with the company goals and culture. I'm very proud of this project because I brought front-line workers into the brainstorming process when the initial discussion with department heads suggested this would never happen. I met initially with the executive committee for input and to learn their key priorities, then met several times individually with each department head to discuss the process and what would best serve their departments. I routed preliminary and final drafts through the executive committee and led consultation through several other committees. Before the deadline, I submitted an excellent plan that is consistent with the company's needs and culture. The plan contributed to an inclusive environment, as demonstrated by the fact that front-line employees have become more involved in decision-making, and morale is at an all-time high.

As a store manager, I had to convince 150 associates during a meeting that to get a bonus, they would have to improve their safety record. Over the next six weeks, we talked about this issue daily, and I communicated my expectation with my management team. After the six-week period, our accident reduction was more than 100 percent, which solidified the associates' bonuses of several hundred dollars each.

Give me an example of a time when you were able to successfully communicate with another person even when that individual might not have personally liked you (or vice versa).

During my time in the theater, I had one director with whom I absolutely did not work well. However, because of my track record, she would assign me as stage director or assistant director. I was usually involved in the day-to-day operations of the play and the details of how the play would be performed. I handled the operation for the play by directing scenes the best way I could and then showing them to her for approval. If she did not like the way a scene worked, I gave her my opinion as to why it should be my way. If we still could not compromise, I would follow her directions to the best of my ability. Understanding that people don't usually have malicious intentions is key, and understanding that you will never be able to convince some people that your way is right is the best way to avoid conflict and still get the job done.

When I first began working at the credit union, I was the youngest member of the staff. An older woman really knew the ropes of the place. When I first got there she barely acknowledged my presence, and through word of mouth I discovered that she thought that I was too young to successfully fulfill my duties because I was so inexperienced. She assumed I was immature. I did my job and took every opportunity to make a good impression. I was a very diligent worker and behaved in a highly professional manner at all times, learning quickly the best way to do things. After about two weeks of the silent treatment from her, she came up to me and told me how impressed she was with me. She told me that I had done an excellent job and was the fastest learner that she had ever seen. She apologized to me for ignoring me and took me under her wing and shared what she knew with me.

Tell of a time when you worked with a colleague who was not completing his or her share of the work. What did you do?

During a group project in college, we had one member who would do no work whatsoever. The project was to compare and contrast four companies in a single industry, so his work was vital. We first discussed the situation and asked for the bare-bones minimum of what we needed from him. We got just below that. As a result we as a group went to the professor and told her our situation, not expecting or requesting action, just informing her of the situation we were dealing with. Then the group split up the noncontributor's work and completed our work collectively on his share. In phase two, in which we analyzed the information and reported how each of our companies fared compared to the others, we did not get a paper from the group member. As a result, we told the teacher that we had our work done and were willing to do the extra paper but that we would rather spend time polishing our own work and not picking up slack. She agreed and said to focus on the three companies we had compiled the most info on while not entirely neglecting the fourth. The papers came out very well, but were understandably weak when comparing the fourth company. The professor understood, and we received the grades we deserved. I was pleased with our teamwork and the way we handled the situation.

Describe a situation in which you had to arrive at a compromise or guide others to a compromise.

My first semester in college, I was a political science major. My introductory government professor had a differing political view from mine. We disagreed on everything, and many classes were filled with criticizing each other's view. However, on one test I answered a question with the view I believe in, and she marked it wrong. So I asked her how an opinion can be wrong, and she said because her opinion is the way she taught it in class. I pointed out that my answer showed I understood the concepts of the question. She agreed, and I also agreed not be so combative in answers on tests. Compromise is the key to problem resolution.

Describe a situation where others you were working with on a project disagreed with your ideas. What did you do?

I was on a project team in a business class in my freshman year in college. The group brainstormed ideas for the video we were assigned to produce, and everyone but me was leaning toward an idea that would be easy. I suggested instead an idea that would be more difficult but would be something different that no other group would be doing. I used my communications skills to persuade the rest of the group to use my idea. During the project, we really learned what teamwork was all about, became a close team, and ended up putting a lot of hard work into the project. All the team members ended up feeling very proud of the video, and they thanked me for the idea for which we earned an A.

Give an example of when you had to work with someone who was difficult to get along with.

As a Resident Advisor, I had another RA who often sought me as a person to confide her complaints to and shared quite a bit of information about activities she'd engaged in that violated the rules. Although I did not mind being a resource for this person, I knew that I could not compromise my integrity or her residents' safety. Although she became very outraged and angry with me, I talked to her about the situation and told her that I would have to tell my supervisor. She eventually understood my responsibility and why I had to come forward with information. She knew that what she had done was against the rules but never realized before I talked to her that she had jeopardized her residents' safety.

Give me a specific example of something you did that helped build enthusiasm in others.

I really enjoy drumming up enthusiasm and assisting others in achieving their goals, whether it's getting involved in an organization as a volunteer—which has frequently provided me with employment—or whether it's through specific event-planning and fund-raising to meet budgetary needs. I also excel at working within a team either as an integral key player or as a leader. I generated enthusiasm for a public-TV auction, where it was becoming harder and harder to get volunteers to make the donation solicitation calls. In my previous PBS auction experience and through learning at conferences, I knew that having three paid part-time telemarketers would not only allow for continuous and accurate communications with a donor, but also the caller had some ownership of the relationship—and more enthusiasm about donating. My superiors were resistant to the idea, but I built enthusiasm by showing them success stories from other stations. They eventually bought the idea, and once we had the telemarketers in place, it was easy to generate enthusiasm in additional volunteers when we needed them.

Describe a time when you got coworkers who disliked each other to work together. How did you accomplish this? What was the outcome?

When I worked for a law firm, my coworkers and I had a huge mailing to complete. We had the choice of working more efficiently as a team or working individually in a much more time-consuming manner. My two coworkers did not care for each other, and they wanted to complete the mail-out on an individual level. When I presented them with the evidence that we would finish at least an hour earlier by working together, they decided that working together was the right path to take. As a result, we finished the mail-out in a short period of time and could work on other tasks that day.

Describe a time when you put your needs aside to help a classmate understand a task. How did you assist him or her? What was the result?

I was studying right before a major finance test. As the class members came into the classroom, a couple of students indicated that they did not understand a concept that I did. Although there was a small section of material that I had not completely mastered, I realized that I knew enough about that section that I could perform well enough to earn a good grade. I knew that the section the other students did not understand was a major portion of the exam since the professor had an interest in this particular subject. I stopped what I was doing to explain to the small group about the Multiplier Effect of Bank Reserves on the overall supply of money. Those students learned enough from what I taught them that they did well on the exam. I missed a few points on the section of material that I had not mastered, but I did well enough to get an A, and the satisfaction I got from teaching others the concept made me feel proud.

Give me a specific example of a time when a coworker or classmate criticized your work in front of others.

Another manager became upset with me since some projects were not being completed. Without discussing the situation with me first, she criticized me in front of one of the employees I directly supervised. I was upset that she made me look bad in front of my worker, but I remained calm and asked her to step into the office so that we could talk about it in more detail. We discussed the problem, and she learned that the noncompletion of the tasks was not my fault. Another manager did not receive his instructions telling him the tasks he needed to complete. After that I learned not to jump to conclusions when dealing with others and that sometimes a miscommunication can lead to a much larger problem. I've learned to get the complete facts.

Time and Project Management

Describe the most complex project you've been involved with.

When I was working as a data-entry examiner in claims, I was asked to participate on a team to help create a manual to document the process for data entry of claims. At the time, documents and training material were scattered across several resource files, but nothing straightforward, simple, and comprehensive had been designed for the insurance company's largest client, the state of Nevada. From the start, I knew this would be a complex project because when we began mapping the decision trees and process, the map grew exponentially, and we found ourselves overwhelmed by the amount of research needed. To handle the project, I broke it down into four main categories and assigned them to individuals to research. I also selected one person to be the master editor and to keep us motivated and on track. I set deadlines so we could pace ourselves over the next few weeks to produce a value-added deliverable. We also rotated the work assignments when completed so we could check each other's work for consistency and hammer out any policy differences and interpretations as they came up. In the end, we finished the 200+ page manual in about three months. All of us were extremely proud of the document we created. If I could do one thing over again, I would have probably made the manual a Web-based document so it could be searched and browsed.

I had to give a marketing presentation while attending community college. The project was about Anheuser-Busch. We were assigned to report on key management personnel (CEO, Chairman of the Board, President, key VPs), divisions and subsidiaries, major products/brands/services, key financials for the most recent year (sales revenue, expenses, total income, net income, sales growth or loss for the last year), market share, key competitors, mission statement, product positioning, and number of employees. The steps I took included visiting the company's Miami branch to interview employees and gather visual aids for the project. I spent considerable time organizing and writing the presentation. Then I spent time reviewing my speech over a period of several days. As a result I was calm while giving the presentation and earned an A for the project. The one additional step I perhaps wish I'd taken would have been to talk to some consumers and storeowners about the product.

My senior research was my most complex assignment. It took two semesters to complete and was made up of many components, including gathering significant amounts of primary and secondary research. I had to make many critical decisions along the way that would affect the outcome of my research. I made these decisions independently with minimal influence from my professor. I was very successful and happy with my final product, an 80-page comprehensive report.

How do you determine priorities in scheduling your time?

I took a time-management course in which I learned to prioritize all tasks on A, B, or C lists. I always try to tackle the A list first. In every working situation, coworkers have always complimented me on how well I manage my time. I enjoy the social atmosphere of the office, but I make it a point not to waste much time on chitchat with colleagues. I've also learned that the average office worker spends about an hour a day handling e-mail. I make it a point not to deal with my e-mail more than once or twice a day, and I filter my messages into folders so I can prioritize the way I deal with them.

Decision-Making

Give an example of a time in which you had to be relatively quick in coming to a decision.

This situation happens often in the IT industry, but one recent example was when we had a core backbone switch die. It died at the worst possible time—during a crunch production period—as they always seem to do, and I needed to get it back up and running quickly. I analyzed the logs and system status, and using my previous experience, I made some quick decisions that rectified the problem and got the equipment back up only minutes later.

Give me an example of a time you had to make an important decision. How did you make the decision?

My sophomore year was about to begin, and I had to decide on a major. I could not waste any more credits figuring out what I was interested in. I took some personality and career assessments to get a better handle on my interests, skills, and values. I talked to faculty in several departments to decide which faculty members I was most comfortable with. I studied the course offerings to see which courses appealed to me the most. I decided on communications studies and feel it is the best decision I ever could have made.

Tell me about a time when you had to make a decision but didn't have all the information you needed.

I had to make a decision recently between two configurations on one of our routers. Time was quickly getting away from me, and I had to have all the equipment back up in a matter of minutes. I chose the configuration that I had the most data on because I knew at least that I could better troubleshoot it if there was a problem. My decision was the right one.

Communication

Describe a time when you had to use your written communication skills to get an important point across.

> *As an administrative coordinator at a resort's convention center, I had a staff of 27. Having such a large staff all working different shifts and having varying schedules meant that meetings could not be held with everyone at one time. I needed to communicate with everyone about important policies and information often, so I came up with the idea of designing a Web page for my staff with written announcements. Each desk assistant was required to check the Web page daily at the beginning of his or her shift. I also sent e-mail communications via a distribution list that kept each desk assistant informed. The one situation that stands out in my mind is a last-minute group that decided to come in a day early with only one day's notice. I had no staff scheduled to check in the group or to organize the keys. I posted an update to the Web page and sent an e-mail. Within four hours, I had the following day completely staffed and desk assistants there to organize room keys for the group members that night.*

Tell of a time when your active listening skills really paid off for you—maybe a time when other people missed the key idea being expressed.

> *When I presented my senior research in college, the members of my major department as a panel questioned me. My grade was determined largely on my ability to answer the questions effectively and smoothly, which depended very much on my ability to listen carefully to what was being asked. I had seen other students slip up when they misunderstood what the panel was asking because they didn't listen well enough. I succeeded in listening well and did well on my presentation.*

Workplace Behavior, Manageability

Give me a specific occasion in which you conformed to a policy with which you did not agree.

> *When I worked at Home Depot as an assistant manager, I was always looking for ways to boost my employees' morale. Unloading trucks is a very routine and physical job and can become very boring and exhausting, so to improve the unloaders' attitude toward their duties and make the best of the situation, I put a radio in the receiving dock. It worked; however, the district manager did not approve of the radio in the workplace even though it did not interfere with any set policy or company objectives. The radio was also out of any areas where customers would hear the music. I did not agree with my DM's decision to remove the radio; however, I understood his point of view once he explained it to me and promptly complied with his request. The employees were not happy that their*

radio was gone, so I found an alternative method of reward and morale boosting by implementing a program in which we provided lunch for the unloaders from any restaurant of their choice if they unloaded the trucks faster than normal. This program succeeded by decreasing their unloading time from 2½ hours to only 1½, a savings in payroll of 8 percent of sales for that shift.

Have you ever had difficulty with a supervisor or instructor? How did you resolve the conflict?

Yes, I had an incident with my Spanish professor. I turned in an essay that she said was too good to be mine. I was honest with her; I told her that I had a native speaker review the essay, but he made very few corrections. However, I had broken the Golden Rule of Spanish Composition: the essay must not even touch the hands of a native speaker. To prove to her that I was capable of producing an essay that exceeded her expectations of a non-native speaker, I offered to rewrite another essay in her office. I earned an A-minus.

What kind of supervisor do you work best for?

I like to work for a supervisor who allows me the autonomy to perform my job to the best of my abilities. I also like constructive criticism and feedback so I can improve myself and the organization. One example was my boss at a hospital. He hired me as an administrative manager because of my administrative and organizational skills. He knew that I had many new ideas and allowed me the opportunity to implement many new programs. Of course, I kept him constantly informed and sought advice when needed. I improved communications in the department by implementing a departmental Web page. I also streamlined the check-in process by preparing the amount of work that could be done the day before. I improved staff morale by implementing an administrative staffer of the month, which led to lower turnover. These are just a few examples. I earned the Outstanding Employee Award for my efforts and unique ideas. I gained not only my boss's confidence and support but his respect as well.

Work Ethic and Performance

Compare and contrast the times when you did work that was above the standard with times your work was below the standard.

I was involved in two group projects in a psychology class. In the first, we had to decide on a research experiment to conduct and garner results from it. The group I was in was not very motivated, and the members wanted to do a simplistic comparison on color preferences of men and women. I felt that project was below the standard I was capable of. For the second project, I proposed a study in which we compared how people of different age ranges valued money. I knew the project would go over well with the teacher and would not be difficult to conduct. I proposed the idea in a way that sounded fun. Instead of collecting data in someplace boring, I suggested we could go to the mall. The group agreed and worked relatively well on the project. Discussion is the key to mediation and was the key to my achieving a second project that I felt was above the standard.

How have you differed from your professors in evaluating your performance? How did you handle the situation?

After I wrote a paper for an English class, my professor told me that I was not doing the paper in the proper format or with the proper content. I went to him and asked if he would help me learn the correct way so that I could succeed with the paper. He did help me, and I ended up doing well in the course.

What are your standards of success in school? What have you done to meet these standards?

In my human-resources management class we were assigned a paper on "Why corporate culture is a practical way to increase income and productivity." All of the literature on the subject was written in the language of Ph.D.s. I asked some other students what they were doing, and they said just writing their opinions and not doing any research to back up the claims. I felt I could do better. I am always willing to ask questions to learn how to perform an assignment successfully. So I worked closely with my professor, who "translated" the academic literature for me, and over time I understood what was being written. Working with the professor's guidance, I turned in a very good paper. Asking questions is one thing I am not afraid to do and realize that without them I will be turning in work that is not as beneficial as it could be.

Give an example of your experience at school or in a job that was satisfying. Give an example of your experience that was dissatisfying.

I turned a dissatisfying experience into a satisfying one when I was on the cross-country team in college and had never run the whole race in under 30 minutes. With only a month left in the season, I decided that I would run the race in 25 minutes. I ran every day to build up my stamina, and in that last race I achieved my goal time of 25 minutes, which was a very satisfying experience.

What do you think it takes to be successful in this career?

It takes the ability to meet every customer with a smile, and a solution—whatever it takes. Though I've worked in a number of industries, I have always been a salesperson and a consistent top producer. Let me elaborate. Early in my career, I sold memberships at a family fitness center. An angry man once came to me demanding a refund. He began yelling at the membership workers and complaining about the swimming program, saying that it was a rip-off. Though the other workers were flustered, I calmly asked the man what was wrong. He that his son had been in swimming lessons for four weeks and was still afraid of the water. Instead of instantly giving him the refund, I offered to personally arrange for private swim lessons for his son for a week, explaining to him that sometimes children react differently to each instructor's teaching techniques. He finally agreed to accept without the refund. After a week of private lessons, his son was no longer afraid of the water and he could swim nearly a lap of the pool. At the end of the lessons, not only did the father sign his child up for another paid session of private lessons, but he also bought a family membership and apologized to me for his behavior the week before.

What is the most significant contribution you made to the organization during a past job?

My organization was undergoing an accreditation process. I developed two detailed accreditation self-evaluation reports that documented how the organization met accreditation standards. These self-evaluations served as the basis for accreditation site visits and enabled all eligible programs to be accredited in record time.

Transition to and From College

How was your transition from high school to college? Did you face any particular problems?

The transition was somewhat challenging for me because I traveled a great distance to attend college. To help myself adapt, I got involved with as many organizations as I could. I also made it a point to get to know my professors. I used my interpersonal communication skills to the best of my ability to make a lot of friends, and college became one of the best experiences of my life despite a beginning that seemed a bit overwhelming.

How has your college experience prepared you for a business career?

I have prepared myself to transition into the workforce through real-world experience involving travel abroad, internship, and entrepreneurial opportunities. While interning with a private organization in Ecuador, I developed a 15-page marketing plan composed in Spanish that recommended more effective ways the company could promote its services. I also traveled abroad on two other occasions in which I researched the indigenous culture of the Mayan people in Todos Santos, Guatemala, and participated in a total language immersion program in Costa Rica. As you can see from my academic, extracurricular, and experiential background, I have unconditionally committed myself to success as an international marketing professional.

Storytelling for Situational and Future-Oriented Interview Questions

The situational question is fairly common in job interviews and is similar to the behavioral question. Instead of asking you how you handled a certain situation in the past, the interviewer asks how you *would* handle the situation in the future. You can answer this kind of question with the same kind of story you would use to answer a behavioral question. Simply explain that this is the story of how you handled the situation previously, and you would expect to use the same skills and knowledge to handle the situation if you are hired for this job.

Occasionally an interviewer will ask a hypothetical question about what you would do if you were hired by the employer, such as what would be the first few things you would do in the job or what suggestions you have for improving the organization. Here, too, you have the option of responding to the question by telling a story from your past experience, but another option is to tell a future story. The future story is different from any other story discussed in this book because it's essentially fiction; it hasn't happened (yet). But you have the opportunity to describe a future scenario in which you would play a major role in meeting the employer's needs and solving its problems. You can paint a vivid picture of what it would be like if you were hired.

Here are some examples of these types of questions and how to answer them:

How would you organize the steps or methods you'd take to define/identify a vision for your team or your personal job function?

> *I believe a good team vision starts first with a strong understanding of the organization's mission. So, my steps would be as follows:*
>
> *First, review my organization's vision.*
>
> *Second, develop some rough ideas of how I would word a team vision statement in preparation for a team meeting to discuss the issue.*
>
> *Third, I would call a meeting of the team and have a discussion of what we do best and how what we do fits with the organization. Then I would discuss the organization's vision and ask for ideas and suggestions for the team's mission. If asked, I would mention some of my thoughts on our team vision.*
>
> *Fourth, following the meeting, I would craft a vision statement—perhaps with the help of one or two other team members—and then distribute it to the team and ask for feedback.*

Fifth, I would finalize the vision statement from the comments and feedback from the team, and then post our vision statement in places where all the team members could see it on a regular basis.

What would a good manager do to build team spirit?

Most importantly, any plan to build team spirit has to be authentic. We've all seen—or experienced—work environments like in Office Space or The Office. Anything less than authenticity will be seen as simply rah-rah—or going through the motions.

A good manager brings the team together—perhaps even a retreat—to foster communications and develop common goals and objectives. During this meeting, the manager should also show how all the team members play a role in making the team successful—and that only by working together and respecting each other can the team fully succeed.

Sometimes, too, when the team is from different departments or backgrounds, it's important for the manager to address this issue from day one, if possible. I was once put on a team with a mix of marketers and accountants and the manager sat us all down and told us a story of a successful competitor and how their accounting team thought like marketers and how their marketers understood the importance of return on investment for new marketing initiatives. The story of a successful competitor helped us realize that we had more in common than we had differences and that we could come together as a team and be successful.

What suggestions do you have for our organization?

After examining several sources, including your company's annual report and Web site, as well as some of your competitors' sources, I see that you have a strong product line with good demographic segments, in a growing industry. I did notice that your competitors seem to direct more of their efforts to the baby-boom market, and while that is certainly a large market for your products, I think you have a great opportunity to expand your target market and increase your market share by marketing your product line to the baby boomers' kids: Generation Y. These teens and preteens are extremely brand-conscious and have a high discretionary income—and you are in a great position to attract them to your product and build a very large core of brand-loyal consumers on top of your existing customer base. In fact, I recently walked by a store display of your wall art and t-shirts centered on 1960s rock-star themes. I expected to see mature folks looking at the products, but what I saw was a group from middle-school age to college age clamoring excitedly around the display. I also know my teenage nieces and nephews have grown up highly influenced by their parents' devotion to The Beatles, The Rolling Stones, and The Beach Boys, and they all own at least one of your products.

For Easy Retrieval from Your Brain's Database, Give Your Stories a Title

To flush out key accomplishments from her clients, resume writer and job search coach Norine Dagliano encourages them to tell her specific stories, guiding them through the SOAR or STAR process. Among the questions she asks to trigger these stories are these:

- What was challenging about that job?
- How have things changed from the time you took the position (or joined the company) to the present?

When teaching interviewing classes or conducting interview coaching, Dagliano teaches clients how to create an "interview cheat sheet." She asks them to draw a big T on a sheet of paper. On the left side of the T, clients write the word "Skill" and on the right side, the word "Story." Dagliano then guides them through the job posting or job description they are targeting to pick out key skills mentioned. She also instructs them to go through their resume to pick out the key skills that they want to talk about in the interview. They then list all these skills on the left side of the T.

Dagliano next coaches clients through the process of thinking through a story to illustrate how they used each skill they have listed—again using the SOAR process. Once they have developed the details of their stories, Dagliano advises them to give their story a title (using as few words as possible) and write that title on the right side of the T on their cheat sheet.

"Once they have the stories worked out," Dagliano says, "they will be ready to answer almost any interview question that comes their way. To prove it, I ask a few typical—and some not so typical—interview questions and coach them on how to use elements of the story in answering. I encourage them to take the cheat sheet to the interview with them and have it with the notepad where they take notes during the interview."

Dagliano notes that our brains have a remarkable ability to locate things in a pinch as long as we have "told" the brain where we have filed them. Dagliano says that if clients draw a blank on how to answer a question, by merely glancing down at their cheat sheet and seeing the story title, their brains will quickly retrieve the details of the story and the best answer.

Compose Your Stories in Writing Before the Interview

by Katharine Hansen and Randall S. Hansen, Ph.D.

Okay, so you're sold on the idea of telling stories in your job interviews. Can you simply think about the stories you want to tell? Sure, but composing written story responses to questions typically asked in job interviews provides a relatively painless way to prep effectively for a job interview.

Based on our research, personal experience, and anecdotal evidence from the college students we have taught, we are convinced that preparing written stories in response to job interview questions will accomplish these goals:

- Increase the interviewee's level of confidence in responding to questions.
- Show evidence of preparedness by providing thoughtful, nonrambling responses.
- Increase the level of relevance by specifically addressing the questions.
- Provide more detail and thoroughness in responding to questions.
- Allow the interviewee to focus more on response delivery in the interview setting.

A number of years ago, we discovered that preparing written answers to job interview questions helped us perform better in job interviews. That discovery prompted us to assign our students to compose responses to frequently asked interview questions. Because this assignment frequently has seemed to enhance performance both in mock interviews and actual job interviews, we turned to two disparate areas of research to understand why the technique was effective. We concluded that the phenomenon is closely related to the Writing to Learn theory.

Interview Preparation

Research by Perry and Goldberg in 1998 suggested that interview preparation is important because interviewing skills were more important than students' background or experience when recruiters were asked about the likelihood that their companies would consider hiring a given student. We can then speculate that students (and other job candidates) who have better interview skills than others may have dedicated more effort to interview preparation than others.

Most career experts agree that few interviewees prepare adequately for interviews. In 1995, Barone and Switzer went so far as to note that, while college students spend in excess of 4,000 hours studying and attending class to prepare for their career, the average interviewee spends less than an hour preparing for a job interview. These experts also agree on the reason for the lack of preparation: job seekers have no idea what questions will be asked in interviews, so they assume there is no way to prepare. Finally, career authors agree that this typical job seeker rationale for lack of preparation is faulty because interview questions, or at least general areas of interview questions, actually can be predicted to some degree. Also, lists of frequently asked interview questions are available in any number of books, articles, and Web sites. See, for example, the Interview Question Database at www.quintcareers.com/interview_question_database/ and lists of interview questions at www.quintcareers.com/interview_question_collections.html.

Agreeing that it is impossible to predict exactly what questions a given interviewer will ask of a job seeker, interviewing guru Carole Martin nevertheless notes that "the secret to success in any interview is preparation." Author Tom Washington points out that since so few job seekers prepare for interviews, those who do will "gain a real edge over others through preparation."

Career experts are virtually unanimous in their view that responses to interview questions should not be memorized but should be prepared, in some fashion, ahead of time.

Since you know that lists of typical interview questions are widely available, you can review them to gain an idea of what types of information the interviewer likely seeks. Taking this advice a step further, you can use these question lists to organize your thoughts about high points you want to share with employers and develop a list of the characteristics that might be needed for success in the position for which you are interviewing. You can then craft stories about these characteristics using the guidelines in chapter 2. You can also engage in verbal mock or rehearsal interviews; however, Janet Emig points out that "writing tends to be a more responsible and committed act than talking." Thus, writing-as-interview-prep includes these suggestions:

- Writing an autobiography, which can reveal areas that you might not want to discuss with an interviewer.
- Practicing describing yourself by citing professional characteristics with examples from school and work experience.
- Writing detailed proof statements/success stories that are tantamount to 30-second commercials about yourself.
- Identifying about 30 accomplishments and writing 100–400 word stories on the top 12 of these, followed by isolating skills demonstrated by each accomplishment.

Writing to Learn

Why are these writing exercises effective in enhancing interview performance? We credit the Writing-to-Learn theory. James Britton, considered by many to be the father of the Writing-to-Learn movement, asserts that writing is learning because writing enables learners to organize their knowledge "and extend it in an organized way so that it remains coherent, unified, reliable." Janet Emig notes that "writing through its inherent reinforcing cycle involving hand, eye, and brain marks a uniquely powerful multi-representational mode for learning." Other scholars expand on Emig's "reinforcing cycle." "It's a physical activity, unlike reading," writes William Zinsser. "Writing requires us to operate some kind of mechanism—pencil, pen, typewriter, word processor—for getting our thoughts on paper." David Joliffe asserts that this physical act of writing compels writers to become "actively involved" with what they're writing about. Through writing, Joliffe says, participants "generate challenging ideas...engage in a substantial process...practice analysis and synthesis...and demonstrate a personal commitment to their ideas...." Suzanne Cherry calls writing "thinking on paper."

Composing written stories in response to interview questions works because it helps candidates learn and remember concepts and content, improve thinking and cognitive abilities, organize their thoughts, enhance communication skills, bolster their self-image, and make connections. The story form is easy to remember because we think in narrative form because our neural networks were shaped in childhood through storytelling.

Demonstrating thoughtfulness and organized thinking is positively associated with interview performance, according to a study by Maurer, Solamon, Andrews, and Troxtel. Noting that cognitive ability in applicants has been shown to be a "strong and consistent predictor of job performance," and, in fact, to predict job performance more "accurately and universally" than other constructs (largely because this ability indicates candidates' ability to rapidly learn job requirements), Huffcutt, Roth, and McDaniel posit that applicants with higher cognitive ability may exhibit greater effectiveness than other candidates in responding to situational and abstract questions. The Writing-to-Learn technique's claims to help its practitioners organize their thoughts and make connections suggests that the Writing-to-Learn approach would be one way to sharpen your communicative abilities for interviewing.

New Research

We tested this Writing-to-Learn approach to interview prep on three sections of a basic marketing class consisting mainly of college juniors, with a small number of sophomores and seniors also participating. Students in the sections who were assigned to complete the written interview-preparation assignment were given a list of 20 common interview questions for college students and asked to submit written responses to each. A local human-resources professional with many years of interviewing experience was recruited to interview and score the participants. He was instructed on how to complete the evaluation forms, but at no time did he know that one group of interviewees had previously prepared written responses to the potential questions and that the other group hadn't. The group that prepared the written responses to the interview questions scored higher on the study's evaluation instrument than the group that did not. Although the difference we saw did not prove to be statistically significant, it might indicate a trend.

Based on the possible trend indication of the study, as well as previous scholarly research dealing with interview preparation and Writing-to-Learn, we are confident of the relationship between written interview preparation and interview success. We are committed to the idea that preparing written answers to common interview questions will make you more confident and allow you to focus your energies on other aspects of the interview while providing detailed yet concise stories in response to questions.

Summary

Stories have long been a natural for job interview responses and provide job seekers with one of their best opportunities to showcase storytelling skills with solid accomplishment narratives. Stories are especially appropriate for behavioral interview questions, which the job seeker can answer using any variation of the situation-action-result formula. Stories, however, are also an effective way to respond to traditional, situational, future-oriented, and yes-or-no questions. This chapter has offered numerous sample storied responses to a wide variety of interview questions.

CHAPTER 8

Telling Stories to Communicate Your Personal Brand

Personal branding, an emerging trend in career-marketing communication, is variously defined as image, reputation, connection, a promise of the unique value of a product (you), and expertise. Randall Hansen, publisher of the career-development Web site Quintessential Careers, writes that "branding is the combination of tangible and intangible characteristics that make a brand unique. Branding is developing an image—with results to match."

Branding (some call it self-branding when talking about individuals) is essential to career advancement because it helps define who you are, in what ways you are a great performer, and why you should be sought out. Branding is about building a name for yourself, showcasing what sets you apart from others, and describing the added value you bring to a situation. Your brand describes your essence and the significance you bring to employers.

Most job seekers are not proactive in establishing and building their career brands, hoping instead to let their actions speak for them when seeking promotions or new jobs. But you can make yourself a much more attractive employee or job seeker by taking the time to master some basic tactics that can help build your career brand. In this book's introduction, Annette Simmons cautioned that when people wonder who you are, "if you don't take the time to give a positive answer to that question, they will make up their own answers—usually negative." The same is true of branding; if you don't brand yourself, others will for you.

Management guru Tom Peters, writing in his book, *The Brand You 50*, states: "Regardless of age, regardless of position, regardless of the business we happen to be in, all of us need to understand the importance of branding. We are the CEOs of our own companies: Me, Inc." He adds, "You're not defined by your job title and you're not confined by your job description."

Branding, especially personal branding, is primarily storytelling, and another advantage of branding yourself is that your story is unique. "When you learn to put words to your unique story, you can use it and the values you've developed to define you in a way that no one can copy," writes Chris Hiliki in *May I Have Your Attention, Please?*

Noting that most people are marketers to some extent, author of popular marketing books Seth Godin (*Purple Cow, The Big Moo, All Marketers Are Liars*) does not believe marketing without stories is possible: "Either you're going to tell stories that move people, or you will become irrelevant," he writes. Organizational storytelling expert Steve Denning similarly notes that "narrative is increasingly recognized as central in branding," and when he refers to a "storied product," he could easily be referencing a job seeker.

Getting your brand story out there raises your visibility and builds your aura as an attractive candidate for hire. Symbiotically, elevating the world's awareness of you creates new opportunities for networking. Increasingly, in the Information Age, success can spring not just from who you know, but also from who knows you and your story.

"Personal branding is about differentiation," writes William Arruda, founding partner and president of the Reach Branding Club. "It's about using what makes you outstanding to stand out from the myriad others who offer seemingly similar services. There are numerous others who compete for the same jobs and clients. Personal branding helps you stand head and shoulders above the competition by highlighting your unique promise of value."

Writing Your Story-Supported Branding Statement

An effective way to begin your personal-branding effort is to develop a very brief branding statement that sums up your value proposition. Tom Peters advises that this statement be just eight words long, while a single sentence is the recommendation of William Arruda and Kristin Dixson, whose free, downloadable workbook on personal branding (www.careerdistinction.com/workbook/) accompanies their book, *Career Distinction*. This branding-statement element will guide your subsequent branding activities and can be used in such media as your resume, Web site, or blog. In their book *Brand Yourself,* David Andrusia and Rick Haskins present a simple formula for a branding statement:

> Skills + Personality/Passion + Market Needs = Branding Statement

It's a great formula, but you can enhance it further with one or more stories that support your statement. You can also compose stories that will help you develop your branding statement.

Why should your branding statement generate and be supported by a story? Chris Hilicki, author of *May I Have Your Attention, Please?*, makes a strong argument: "When you build your brand identity on your true experiences, you will bring to the world the only thing that no one else can. Your true story conveys your unique value and is the "strongest foundation of your brand identity," Hilicki contends.

Exercises and Examples

What stories should you tell to brand yourself? Try this exercise: Take about a minute to write down what you are most known for. In what area(s) can you offer yourself as an expert? Ideally you are considered an expert in some area of your career or professional life, but hobbies and interests can be fair game, too. Now, compose a brief story about your expertise in each area—perhaps telling how your expertise has made a difference or changed someone's life. Note that branding statements are usually written in the third person.

Here's an example from my partner, Randall Hansen, that brands his career as a college professor:

> *Branding statement:* Dr. Randall Hansen is an educator who thrives on empowering people to achieve their personal success.
>
> *The story behind the statement:* Education is not about lecturing; it is not about describing the steps or procedures of something—it is about opening someone's mind to learning, and that's what I am all about. It's about turning the helpless or lost person into someone who is self-actualized and can find his or her own way out of the situation. For example, I had a graduating senior who was feeling great pressure to find a job, and while he knew some basics of job hunting, he was allowing circumstances to overwhelm him. I did not need to lecture him about the best methods of finding a job, nor did I have to create or edit his resume; instead, I served as the calming voice in his head that mentored him and allowed him to truly start his job search. Because I worked one-on-one with him and provided guidance and support when he needed it, he was able to develop and follow up on several job leads that eventually led to a job offer that was the perfect opportunity for him. And by accomplishing this task on his own, he not only was able to land this job, but he also now has the skills, confidence, and ability to move forward in his career and conduct future job searches with ease.

If the preceding exercise didn't provide enough food for thought, consider Hilicki's challenge: Write your autobiography in 300 words. Another exercise, which Hilicki attributes to business coach Scott Jeffrey, is to imagine you have only 24 hours to live; "What would your message be to the world and who would your audience be?" Also think about Hilicki's belief that "the best brands are built from true stories that have been picked apart and analyzed and edited."

Story Types You Can Use as a Basis

Ponder the following types of stories as the potential basis for your statement. Then pick apart, analyze, and edit your results:

- A story that demonstrates your understanding of and experience with your audience's needs (in most cases, your audience will be employers or clients).
- A story that shows how you are uniquely qualified to meet your audience's needs.
- A story that illustrates how passionate you are about your field.
- A story that exemplifies the validity of your point of view or school of thought.
- A story that demonstrates that your previous audiences hold you in esteem, respect you, trust you, and contribute to your credibility and excellent reputation.
- A story that illustrates alliances and partnerships that support you.
- A story that describes life-changing events and how they've shaped your values and beliefs.
- A story that reflects recurring patterns in your life/career and what those patterns mean.
- A story that shows how you fit in with the history of your field.
- A story that illustrates how you've positively changed people you've worked with and/or organizations you've worked for.
- A story that exemplifies how you've contributed to the success of people you've worked with and/or organizations you've worked for.
- A story that demonstrates a pioneering idea you've developed.
- A story that shows that people seek you out for your skills and expertise.
- A story that explains how your work has developed and improved.
- A story that includes an award, honor, accolade, testimonial, or other positive quotation that exemplifies your value proposition.

- A story that illustrates that you consistently seek continuing education and professional development to enhance your value to your audience.
- A story about volunteer or philanthropic work that shows what you are passionate about.
- A story that demonstrates the roots of your ethics and values.

Examples of Story-Supported Branding Statements

Here's a branding statement I developed about teaching at the college level:

> *Branding Statement:* As a teacher, Katharine Hansen strives to create an active, exciting learning community in which she is one of the learners. She may lead and facilitate while providing content and expertise, but she is, above all, a learner. Her greatest source of pride in her teaching career comes from having learned, grown, and improved as an instructor.
>
> *The story behind the statement:* In my first semester of teaching, I was a horrible teacher. I stood in front of the class and read my notes. As terrible as I was, one student, named Ted, saw something in me. I could have quit since I was so terrible, but Ted's belief in me encouraged me to keep going. I've improved every semester and am now well liked and respected among students. *[explains how work has developed and improved]*

More examples:

> *Branding statement:* Amy Addison is a rising public-relations professional who relentlessly pursues continuing education and will not rest until she has gained the optimal and most well-rounded qualifications.
>
> *The story behind the statement:* I have started on a program of self-directed study in business communication to prepare for my goal to graduate from a public-relations program that I have identified. I am also preparing my credentials and reviewing my notes from the marketing, financial analysis, and economics courses that I have studied so I can take tests to exempt me from these courses and finish my degree faster and therefore make a greater contribution to my employer's PR agency and its clients. *[illustrates consistent pursuit of continuing education and professional development to enhance value to audience]*

Branding Statement: Frank Jameson is a marketing guru who generates innovative and profitable solutions to marketing problems.

The story behind the statement: Give me a marketing problem and I will produce one or more innovative solutions that result in higher stakeholder satisfaction while achieving the organization's profitability goals. For example, while working as marketing manager for Nabisco, I took over a sagging cookie and cracker division that was losing market share and shelf space, and within a year returned the brand to its position as the dominant brand in its category. While the sales and profits results speak for themselves, it was the multipronged attack of working with the marketing staff, the sales force, and our channel partners that I am most proud of. I collaborated with my marketing team to develop a plan that was easy for our sales force to implement and that reinvigorated our channel partners. The plan involved updating some of the tired packaging of our flagship brands, developing some unique cross-promotional strategies among products in different categories, reinventing our entire product-line Web presence, offering our consumers multiple connections with our brands, and strengthening our relationships with our channel members by guaranteeing them more store traffic and increased sales. The result of this effort was a more loyal and involved consumer base, higher morale among our sales force, increased enthusiasm from our channel partners, and high praise from top management and our stockholders for recouping the lost luster of the brands and increasing both sales and profitability. *[illustrates how he has positively changed the people and/or organization he worked for]*

For a career changer:

Branding Statement: As an aspiring special-education teacher, Tricia Turkelson offers calm steadiness and patience while setting high expectations for students to prepare them for life beyond school. She believes it is a disservice to students to do anything less. As a career changer, she is mature, imbued with life experience, and clear about her career aspiration: to make a difference in the lives of students with disabilities.

The story behind the statement: One example of making a difference is when I worked with an emotionally disturbed student during my field experience. He lacked social skills. I worked with him three times weekly to reinforce the idea that he should ask to join a group of other students. Eventually he built up the confidence to

> ask others to be a part of the group. I polished my interpersonal skills long before returning to school to train as a special-education teacher. The patience and communication skills that I developed during 15 years of managing staff as an office manager will make me a better teacher than I would have been had I started earlier in my life.

Once you establish your brand, carry it through your career-marketing communication. You can use it on your resume (in this case using first-person voice rather than third-person), in an online or print portfolio, on your personal Web site, in your blog (see page 174), on networking/business cards, and more. Also consider enhancing your branding by offering yourself to the media for your expertise, speaking in public, generating visibility in professional organizations, serving as an adjunct instructor or consultant at a college or university, writing articles for publication, and serving on advisory boards and boards of directors.

Personal Branding, "Googlability," and Your Storied Online Presence

Chapter 6 on portfolios touched on the growing trend in which employers seek information on candidates by looking them up on Internet search engines and the accompanying importance of creating and managing your online presence. To underscore that importance, *BusinessWeek* has reported that 87 percent of recruiters use Google and social networks (such as LinkedIn) to decide about candidates. Google searches are so crucial to recruiters that they hold training classes, write manuals, and share secrets on discussion boards about exotic Google search strategies to find candidates. "In executive circles, having a LinkedIn profile is becoming as expected as being searched on Google," says CEO coach Deborah Wile Dib. "Not having one is almost a negative." A 2007 survey conducted by the Institute for Corporate Productivity revealed that 65 percent of business professionals are clicking and connecting via personal and professional social networking Web sites, with 35 percent of them reporting they use networks to assist them in finding a job.

Keep in mind, though, that employers and recruiters aren't just looking for your "Googlability"—how many times your name pops up in a search. They're also interested in how positive your online image is. Thus, be very careful about how you project your story online. The Internet is a highly public medium, and personal information floating out there in cyberspace could unfortunately work against you. *BusinessWeek* reported that 35 percent of surveyed employers have eliminated candidates based on online information.

You can pump up your online presence through branded storytelling in a variety of venues. But it's not the means of delivering an online presence that is most important; it's the content, and specifically, the story-supported personal-branding content. Dib notes that "companies and recruiters are looking for passive candidates and active candidates with strong brands—clearly defined value propositions and differentiators. They are looking for fit. They are looking for authenticity and passion—the courage of a candidate to be real."

What better way to be real than by telling your own compelling story? Following are some media in which you can do so.

Social/Business Networks and Micro-blogging

Many recruiters and job seekers connect though online business and social networks. The big three are

- **LinkedIn** (www.linkedin.com), with at least 25 million registered users, the most businesslike of the three; average user age is 39.
- **MySpace** (www.myspace.com/), with at least 114 million registered users, the most social of the three and especially growing in popularity with users over age 25.
- **Facebook** (www.facebook.com), with at least 124 million registered users, falls between businesslike and social and is wildly popular with college-age and new-grad users but growing rapidly among those age 25+.

Recruiters, who cite these networks along with the people search engine ZoomInfo (www.zoominfo.com/), like these venues because they can use them to learn about prospective candidates, as well as find out who else knows these prospects. These and other social-networking sites are exploding. Wikipedia lists more than 100 social-networking sites, and those are just the "notable" ones. Recruiters are using them to find candidates, while job seekers are using some of the sites to get found. Another trend is micro-blogging at tremendously popular sites such as Twitter (http://twitter.com/)—telling folks in no more than 140 characters what the user is doing at any given moment.

Candidates that recruiters actually source from social networks still represent a small percentage of the total, but as Kevin Wheeler writes on Electronic Recruiting Exchange, "Recruiting is moving rapidly from a find 'em and screen 'em to a court 'em, stay in touch with them, and sell them profession. These networks will power that charge."

A major advantage is that most of these networks provide an opportunity to build a profile on the networking site, thus giving you a chance to engage in storied personal branding. Let your profile tell your story in a lively, exciting way that truly reflects your personality.

Jim Randall of The Raconteur (www.raconteur.ca/) describes a process he takes clients through that can easily apply to crafting a profile for social-networking sites. The following components can help you create an engaging story on social networking sites:

- **Who you are:** Develop this component using your own authentic voice. You may want to draw from your Quintessential You story (see chapter 1).
- **What you do:** A good way to frame this part of your story, Dib notes, is to think of how you've made a difference for your employers. What outcomes would not have been possible for your employer without your initiatives?
- **How you do it:** Offer stories, and when possible, quantified proof of how effectively you have performed.
- **What you want to be:** Paint a word picture that shows your potential.
- **Your value proposition:** Incorporate your branding statement into your profile story.
- **Your commitment:** Express your passion for what you do.

Here are some examples of great social-networking profiles that tell at least part of the stories of the people behind them (registration at LinkedIn may be required to see these). Deb Dib shared these in an article about LinkedIn on JobHunt.org (www.job-hunt.org/executive-job-search/linkedin-for-executives.shtml):

- Jason Alba: www.linkedin.com/in/jasonalba
- Paul Mullen: www.linkedin.com/in/paulmullenceo
- Meg Guiseppi: www.linkedin.com/in/megguiseppi
- Mark Beckford: www.linkedin.com/in/mbeckford
- Paul Copcutt: www.linkedin.com/in/paulcopcutt
- Deb Dib: www.linkedin.com/in/debdib

Blogging

Where a dedicated careerist of old constructed a job-seeking identity through a resume and a few other printed materials disseminated to audiences that seem puny by today's standards, postmillennial upwardly mobile types are establishing their career identities to vast global audiences using tools such as blogs (short for "Web logs"). And recruiters are responding. Case in point is the notion of the blog as a replacement or accompaniment for a resume. Sarah E. Needleman reported on the Career Journal site that Ryan Loken, a Walmart Stores, Inc., recruitment manager, had filled an estimated 125 corporate jobs by reading blogs.

Internet consultants Michael Heraghty and Gerald Adams call blogs "a narrative form optimized for the web," and blogs are unquestionably storytelling devices in which one's story can unfold via regularly posted entries and also be told on a bio or "About Me" page, such as in these examples:

- Rich Page: http://rich-page.com/about/
- "nahliz:" http://nahliz.blogspot.com/search/label/hire

"Once you have a clear idea of who you are and what you want to do, you can start to tell the universe and attract the people who you would like to work with, talk their language, and sell your future," writes *Blogging for Beginners* author Margaret Stead.

Examples of individuals with a well-branded online presence for themselves or their businesses include the following:

- Career Impact Strategist Lydia C. Fernandes, who notes on her eponymous site (http://lydia.c.fernandes.googlepages.com/) that her story is still unfolding.
- Social networking, Internet marketing, and new media expert Jennifer Goodwin, whose branded story at ThatJenGirl (www.thatjengirl.com/) focuses on her two passions: making money on the Internet and being green, organic, and holistic (and teaching others to do the same).
- "Chief Happiness Officer" Tina Su, who relates at her site Think Simple Now (http://thinksimplenow.com/) that she "left a high-paying job to pursue my passion, and have dedicated my full-time attention to studying the fields of personal transformation, fulfillment, healthy living, and human potential."
- Entrepreneurs with something to say about the world of medicine, such as Bob Hawkinson, author of *The Joy of Diabetes,* who writes at the Web site of the same name, "I was lucky enough to be proclaimed diabetic in

1963 and it's been a cake-walk ever since...yeah right." And Trisha Torrey, who became an advocate for patients (through her site at www.everypatientsadvocate.com/) after she was misdiagnosed with cancer.

- Young entrepreneurs who got an early start on their branded online presence, such as Lily Capehart, whose story is told on the Web site Lizard-Ville (www.lizard-ville.com/): Lily "discovered she can 'hypnotize' lizards at the age of 10 and began to dress up and pose the lizards in miniature sets." Similarly, Jason O'Neill, on the site Pencil Bugs (www.pencilbugs.com/), relates that "When I was 9 years old, I had an idea to make a product that I could sell at a craft fair. ... I started thinking about ways to make homework just a little more fun. That's when I came up with the idea for Pencil Bugs."
- Comedians and humorists who project snarkiness in their online presence, such as Chad Riden (www.chadriden.com/) and Ben Rosenfeld (www.bigbencomedy.com/), whose site announces "Ben is an egomaniac who can't share the spotlight with anyone. After he got booed at karaoke for the umpteenth time, Ben realized he had only two choices: performing stand up or playing tennis—and he can't play tennis drunk."

In chapter 6, you saw Web addresses for some good examples of storytelling online portfolios. At http://brandego.com/gallery.php, you can see portfolios that rise to the next level—branded portfolio/blog combos that tell stories.

Story-supported personal branding should be at the heart of your efforts to propel your career, with consistent branding pervading your resume, cover letter, portfolio, interview responses, and all career-marketing communication. Let your brand support your story, and your story support your brand.

Summary

Personal branding, an increasingly important aspect of the job search, is essentially storytelling. Crafting a personal branding statement that is supported by a story creates a consistent message about your value to employers. You can then apply your branding to an online presence that enables employers to find you at social-media venues (such as LinkedIn and Facebook) and blogs, as well as perhaps on your own Web site and online portfolio.

Part 3

Continuous Career Storytelling

CHAPTER 9

Propel Your Career Through On-the-Job Storytelling

Up to now, this book has focused on telling stories to help you enter organizations. This chapter, in contrast, discusses telling stories in the workplace. As you've seen in the foregoing chapters, telling stories about your ability to adapt to change is important to your career advancement, but being able to tell stories that propel and communicate change in the workplace is even more powerful. As author Peg Neuhauser writes, "If an organization's goal is to become more adaptive and flexible in dealing with change, one of the first things that the people in the organization must do is face the fact that there will be change and start telling stories about it."

This kind of storytelling can also become part of a wonderfully self-perpetuating cycle: You tell stories that drive change. When you seek a promotion or your next job, you are then able to tell stories about how you used storytelling to communicate or propel change. You can also use stories to help you make sense of change and cope with its stress.

Stories to Lead and Communicate Organizational Change

Growing numbers of scholar-practitioners have published books in recent years advocating storytelling for various uses within organizations—including to catalyze change. Among these are Stephen Denning with his 2001 book *The Springboard,* his 2007 volume, *The Secret Language of Leadership,* his 2005 *Leader's Guide to Storytelling*, and his 2004 *Squirrel, Inc.,* which touts storytelling as a technique for promoting organizational change and is told in story form. Among eight types of organizational storytelling that Denning describes are "a story to ignite action" and "a story to lead people into the future," including guidelines for crafting a "springboard story" designed to spark organizational change.

In her 2006 book, *Wake Me When the Data Is Over*, Lori Silverman presents chapters from a broad cross-section of organizational-storytelling experts on using story in day-to-day organizational operations (in such areas as financial management, leadership, and project management), as well as strategically and to propel organizational transformation.

Stories, Denning asserts, are far more effective in driving change than the "mechanistic analysis" embodied by charts, graphs, and bullet points. In *The Springboard*, Denning describes his experiences in using stories to help people and organizations to effect change:

> *I found that a certain sort of story enables change by providing direct access to the living part of the organization. It communicates complicated change ideas while generating momentum toward rapid implementation. It helps an organization reinvent itself. Storytelling gets inside the minds of the individuals who collectively make up the organization and affects how they think, worry, wonder, agonize, and dream about themselves and in the process create—and re-create—their organization. Storytelling enables the individuals in an organization to see themselves and the organization in a different light and accordingly take decisions and change their behavior in accordance with these new perceptions, insights, and identities.*

Narrative is effective in motivating change based on storytelling's common roots in all cultures, notes Robert Dickman in an academic journal article. If you can tell the stories that are shared throughout the corporate culture, Carl Rhodes writes in *The Qualitative Report,* you can also change the stories—thus instigating organizational rebirth.

Examples abound of the ways organizations use stories to communicate about change. Scholars Charlene Collison and Alexander Mackenzie report that a major British public utility used story as part of a change process to create images of new directions and career options in the minds of workers. In another company that Brian Brittain, John Swain, and Janice Simpson describe in *Ivey Business Journal Online*, a CEO used story to illustrate his ability to grasp his employees' gut-level reaction to industry-changing technology. By demonstrating through storytelling that he felt their pain while also painting a clear picture of what the future story would be like, he enabled his employees to envision and embrace the technology's potential. A restaurant chain that planned to open 200 new stores in a two-year period prepared to address the change challenge presented by rapid growth by turning to storytelling to enculturate new hires, Nancy Breuer observes in *Workforce* magazine.

Stories that show transformation can become metaphors for desired change in the audience, scholars Michael Humphreys and Andrew D. Brown note. That kind of transformation is illustrated in these examples:

A faculty member tells her colleagues at a university—plagued with crumbling infrastructure, environmental issues, and stagnant leadership—a very different story of the situation at her alma mater. She hopes the portrayal of how such problems can be solved will inspire a "just imagine…" response in her audience:

> *I recently attended a reunion at my alma mater, Eckerd College, a liberal-arts college of about 1,700 students founded in 1958. A new president, Donald R. Eastman, arrived at the school three years ago. At the reunion in that, his first year, he unveiled a campus master plan that called for a complete rebuilding of almost every residential and classroom building more than 30 years old and eliminating cars from the center of campus.*
>
> *During the past three years the college has significantly improved the landscaping on campus. In place of wet areas and drainage problems, there are now ponds with thriving communities of wading birds and plants. In place of sand spurs, there is now a world-class soccer field and a student recreation area called "South Beach," where you can sunbathe, play volleyball, and watch your classmates kayak or sail by. There are beautiful trees, shrubs, and flowers everywhere.*
>
> *They have placed a "freshman parking" lot at the perimeter of campus as the first step in the new parking plan.*
>
> *Also in the past three years, they have built a new library and a new dorm, and they are breaking ground on a second new dorm that will soon be open. The next step is to start rebuilding the existing dorms (about 34 beds each) one at a time. The next academic building in line is science, an estimated $20 million project.*
>
> *The college's endowment stands at $25–30 million, where it has been for many years. There were no plans for any of the improvements described above before the new president came.*
>
> *I see an administration there that aggressively seeks out problems; searches for real, long-term solutions; and successfully finds the money to implement them.*

A speech pathologist inspires younger colleagues with a story of how she sees their mutual patients:

> *I know that your education has not prepared you properly for what you see every day. I know from when I worked with head-trauma cases how harrowing it is to see someone near your own age injured in a car or motorcycle accident who is just never going to walk again, never going to talk again, never going to eat again, and literally will be in a vegetative state for the next 50 years. But you will also encounter patients who are resilient heroes. I have a patient who was born with no lower jaw. This little girl comes from an amazing, loving town, where she is surrounded by teachers and a delightful father. And she's so spunky. To me, she's on the upswing. She has a talking board, and we plan to teach her dad to sign better. And so I don't get burned out on that. I get very hopeful and tenacious. I*

think some people might get burned out, but to me, there's a great deal of hope and many tenacious, resilient people.

A new IT manager tells his staff of 10 technicians, who are frustrated by their 24/7 on-call rotation, how he addressed this type of stress at his former place of employment. In telling the story, the new manager enables the team to envision how he intends to improve their own situation:

The last team I managed was a lot like you guys and was going through many of the same frustrations you are when I came in. They were doing tedious, time-consuming work, running around fixing telecom problems based on a 24/7 on-call rotation. The first thing I did was get the group together, as I am with you now, to find out exactly what their issues were. I interviewed each of them as a group and individually. I realized that, just as it is with you, the biggest issue was the shifting on-call rotations. The schedule would be set up one week, and then the very next week it would change, because somebody wanted a change, and the manager would change it.

I set up a schedule for the entire calendar year. My only rule was that if you wanted to make a change, you had to work out a deal with one of your teammates to swap. So, I as the manager took myself out of the equation of making the changes; I let the team members figure it out. Sure, there were a lot of grumblings upfront because people could see six months in advance that they would be on-call over Christmas. But the benefit was that they knew that six months in advance, and if they wanted to make some changes or adjustments to the schedule, they could do that—it was their responsibility.

I also added a little fun and playfulness to the environment. I set up a putting green and invented a game called "Putting for Product." Team members came to ask for a piece of equipment—whether a $2 patch cord or a $50,000 piece of equipment. I gave them three free putts. If they sunk one of the three putts, they could take the product no questions asked. If they missed, they'd have to pay a dollar into our candy fund and putt again. Or, they could bypass all that and hire the local golf pro, one of the guys in the office who was really good at golfing, and pay him a dollar to shoot the first round for them. It was a great setting for having conversations, too. We also set up a fishbowl out in the main area so team members could acknowledge and recognize each other's achievements. At the end of the month, at our team meeting, I'd go through this fishbowl, and the person with the most acknowledgments would be acknowledged and receive prizes such as movie passes or coupons for the concession stand. Or, you could trade your prize, but it was like "Let's Make a Deal," so you didn't know what you were trading for. It could be something really nice like clocks and watches, or silly things like gag gifts and pencils.

We also had the management team cook full breakfasts with scrambled eggs and pancakes for the winning team member and three teammates of their choice.

So it was a really neat type of environment that we were creating, trying to lighten up the mood of the group. The team became more comfortable with the challenges they faced. The fun and playfulness really eased the tension that the team felt from the on-call rotation.

Promote Yourself Through Storytelling

Storytelling to advance your career within your organization works much the same way it does when you seek to enter a new organization. Neuhauser notes that employers tend to "reward and promote" employees who demonstrate they can handle change well. When you want to propel your career within an organization, you need to become a story collector.

Keep a record of everything you do that enhances your organization's bottom line, shines a positive light on your organization or department, creatively and innovatively solves organizational problems, and shows your loyalty and commitment to your employer. And, of course, as emphasized in chapter 2, record everything you do that demonstrates how well you have led, communicated, or adapted to change within your organization.

Track Your Accomplishments

The minute you begin a new job, start tracking your accomplishments. Keep a story log in a little notebook, on index cards, in a computer database, on a small tape recorder, or on your handheld device. It's important to collect this data as your accomplishments occur and compose them in story form because most people have a hard time dredging up stories of their past accomplishments and achievements. At key times, such as when a promotion opportunity arises, they're frequently not even convinced they have any accomplishments worth sharing. But everyone has, and anyone who wants to advance on the career ladder should be prepared to articulate achievements beyond the day-to-day tasks he or she performed on the job.

Accomplishments are the points that really help sell you to an employer, much more so than everyday job duties, whether you are selling your qualifications to an employer for the first time or seeking to move up. In the interview she did with Quintessential Careers, career counselor Michelle Watson noted that "employers are seeking success stories." They want to know that you are a problem-solver, a mover and a shaker, a contributor to the organization, and someone who shows initiative. Although promotions are not always based on your past performance, you can certainly make a much better case for a promotion by telling detailed stories about your past successes. Those who get results get ahead.

Expressing your accomplishments in story form using any of the numerous story frameworks throughout this book is a huge advantage because your compelling, engaging story will be memorable to the manager making the promotion decision, whereas the people who aren't telling stories might be forgotten. You will be far more confident, convincing, and persuasive than your competitors who merely list accomplishments—or believe they have no accomplishments. The decision-maker will get to know and trust you through your stories, which may also help you establish the emotional connection that will inspire him or her to invest in your success.

Prompts for Brainstorming Accomplishment Stories

If you haven't tracked your accomplishment stories to date, use the following prompts to brainstorm all those terrific things you did. Develop accomplishments stories that set you apart from others who might be competing for advancement.

- What special things have you done to set yourself apart? How have you done the job better than anyone else did or than anyone else could have done?
- What have you done to make the job your own?
- How have you taken the initiative? How have you gone above and beyond what was asked of you in your job description?
- What are you most proud of in your job?
- What problems have you solved?
- How can you weave into your story tangible evidence of your accomplishments: material from your annual performance reviews, glowing quotes from colleagues, complimentary memos or letters from customers, publications you've produced, products you've developed, and software applications you've written?
- Consider the "PEP Formula" (Profitability, Efficiency, and Productivity) as another way to tell your story. How did you contribute to profitability, such as through sales increase percentages? How did you contribute to efficiency, such as through cost-reduction percentages? How did you contribute to productivity, such as through successfully motivating your team?

We're taught when we're young that modesty is a virtue, but if no one knows how great you are, you simply won't get ahead. Be a known quantity. Sell yourself with stories of your successes, and let the decision-makers know that you seek advancement. Send your boss regular e-mails or memos with stories of your accomplishments and results. Tell these stories verbally in informal and social situations. It's especially important to toot your own horn with stories when you don't see your boss often, particularly if you telecommute or work in a different location from your supervisor.

The following are examples of stories that workers could tell their bosses to increase their chances of advancement:

I have helped shift the focus of our HR department from a transactional one to more of a developmental and proactive approach. Early on, performance issues kept coming up that should have been dealt with much sooner. It was clear to me that we needed to be more proactive and developmental in our HR services to employ best practices and build managers' supervisory skills by designing systems, processes, and tools to simplify and clarify their HR responsibilities. I also began to meet monthly with department heads and department administrators, a practice that has been extremely helpful in addressing emerging issues. The result is an increased commitment to quality supervision across the organization, more efficiency, increased effectiveness on the part of supervisors, and problems being dealt with more proactively.

My boss went on medical leave just as we were starting to wrap up a three-year comprehensive plan. In addition to just getting up to speed on the basics of the job, I was doing data presentations, monitoring agencies that reported to us, and ensuring that expenditure reports were accurate. I had to quickly pick up on the various service categories, understand which agencies provide what services, and prioritize resource allocation. My supervisor ended up taking 12 weeks of leave, so I was running the show. I called my supervisor from time to time for some advice, but I organized and ran the meetings, provided support for other meetings, went out to the agencies, figured out how to do all of the monitoring, ensured that all the reports were in on time, made sure other reports were in on time, and developed good relationships with the agencies. I couldn't have anticipated all of the things that would be happening during the time my supervisor was out. I was essentially working two positions.

Using Storytelling to Cope with the Stress of Change

In July 2006, *BusinessWeek* published a cover story on company mistakes and failures, in which author Jena McGregor listed sharing personal stories of failure as a best practice in dealing with mistakes. "If employees hear leaders discussing their own failures," McGregor writes, "they'll be more comfortable talking about their own." The cover story features several sidebars in which executives describe their favorite mistakes. Mistakes and failures can, of course, be a great source of learning when future changes roll around, as in this sample story:

Two years after I came to the company, we instilled a process in which we started to become a 24/7, 365-day-a-year work organization, supporting the company's software worldwide. We had four global centers, three in the U.S. and one in Europe. The idea was to move the work according to time zones. When East Coast business hours were over, the work was moved to the Midwest center, and so on. The process didn't work well. Things were not getting done because the volumes were growing. When the work was moved over, someone new would pick it up and learn the issue from scratch, causing a delay in solving the problem. Our backlog of issues went above 10,000, and we became literally a reactive call center that just greased the squeaky wheels. We went back to something a little more in line with what customers needed where we owned all of our work. But now we've started a whole new globalization initiative, and all of a sudden the process seems to very closely mimic the time-zone-related process that totally blew up. But I knew that I had to somehow sell the initiative to my team because without any kind of buy-in, it would fail from the start. So it has been very demotivating for me, and I had a lot of struggles with it because I knew that the workload for my engineers would dramatically increase, and of course that would demotivate them. I knew I would start having attrition. Team members would say, "What the heck? I'm leaving. This is crap."

So as a manager, I had to be very flexible to this change. But I did it. I got my people encouraged and feeling good about it, and it actually wasn't quite as bad as the first time around. I had to step up to that and say, "Okay, we know the problems that we had before with this, so let's do something now to see if we can make some changes to move on." As a manager with my global team, I decided to have a few meetings in which we came to an agreement that we would evenly distribute workloads globally, based on the process at hand. The engineers that I manage are seeing that I'm committed to them, and knowing that the process didn't work before, trying to implement changes to help it work this time around.

Mistakes and failures comprise, of course, just one kind of organizational change, but the concept of people, whether executives or anyone else in the organization, including you, telling stories to cope with the stress of change, is the same concept.

Guided by a storytelling activity in a group setting designed by Darl Kolb of the University of Auckland, New Zealand, longtime employees of an organization about to undergo change shared stories of previous changes with less-senior employees. All the workers subsequently expressed lower than expected levels of anxiety and apprehension and less resistance to change. The looming change didn't seem as radical when compared with those changes described by some of the old-timers.

Research by Suzanne O'Hara in *Career Development International* shows that stories help workers make sense of change and undergo a shift in their own understanding of the need for change. Stories show how the change will happen, as David Fleming reports in an article on using narrative for leadership. Scholar Steven S. Taylor describes how stories illustrate what the future will look like once the change is accomplished. The process of reviewing the organization's old stories and creating new ones helps organization members learn to adapt to change, Taylor writes.

More Examples of Change Stories

Smart organization members who understand Fleming's assertion that "a thriving organization sees its mission as an ever-emerging story with all the necessary twists and turns" will tell stories like the following to make sense of change and learn to cope and adapt:

> *On a project I was working on, I needed the help of an analyst in evaluating a work process I was trying to change. The analyst could not understand why incoming pieces of mail in my work area were not being scanned as electronic documents, which is standard practice across the organization. He assumed I hadn't had proper training and was mismanaging the process, but in actuality, the process was new and foreign for the satellite office I was working in. In an e-mail to the analyst, I described the background and rationale for why the processes were different, explaining that priorities, resources, management style, and availability of resources were very different in the satellite offices. The way I wrote the e-mail had to be nonoffensive, neutral, and objective because the analyst had responded to me in a dismissive manner. Ultimately, I convinced the analyst that I needed more of his attention and dedication to address the work process.*

> *Much of human resources requires influencing others to make changes. An excellent example is the way in which I've persuaded managers and supervisors to conduct annual performance evaluations, which wasn't the case when I was hired. I talked with supervisors and managers regarding the value of this responsibility, convened a task force, and designed an evaluation tool for the staff that has consistent criteria, is tied to the organizational goals and values, and is easy to use. I provided training and led conversations with the executive committee to foster support company-wide. The result is that all continuing employees and many temporary employees have received annual performance appraisals for several years.*

> *To bring attention to the growing social problems in my region during a time of high unemployment, I proposed that we do what many of the participants in my temporary employment program were doing to deal with the stress, which was to have a party. A number of other service groups participated, and with our combined effort we had a daylong celebration that included a parade and activities and entertainment throughout the day at a civic park. A union group organized a parade, and another built the staging locations in the park. Through the media, I*

put out requests for donations to make the party work, and I received a donation of two tons of potatoes, which we used to make potato soup. Other organizations, such as church groups, began joining in, and soon we had a large group of volunteers, and the party served more than 7,000 people. It was a success in that it drew attention to the plight of the residents and acknowledged the "elephant in the room" known as unemployment and economic hardships while it gave us a much-needed opportunity to blow off steam.

During a time of change in our company, we had various situations where processes/ways of thinking needed to be changed. I had five managers reporting to me. During a meeting, I laid out what the company was trying to accomplish and then asked for opinions/feedback from each of them. During this meeting I also described the goal so the staff could understand the whole picture. They had questions/concerns, but once we talked through them, they were able to understand our challenge and came on board with the direction we were going in.

I used to not handle change very well. I'm a very routine person. Everything had to be routine for me. The second something got thrown off, it threw off my routine. At the theme park where I work, I was moved to a completely different location with a different environment. I was at a stadium location, with a 14-member staff and a very controlled, outlined, and specific setting. Then I was shifted over to the park's rides area with a staff of 100 people. Everything was always changing. The volume was higher, and there were more people to deal with. I was forced to really have to change. I didn't know how to change and hoped to just assimilate. That change really did throw off my whole routine. When management finally sat me down to explain that I had to change, they broke it down into a process that I was able to understand. I could mentally build the steps in the process—build a picture to make the adjustment. Otherwise, I would've never really adjusted. I probably wouldn't even still be there if I hadn't. All the changing roles I've had have helped me develop a different perspective on dealing with the change. And now you can change me on a whim at work. I can make the adjustment quickly and move forward without having to sit down and analyze how the change fits into my routine.

Katharine's Own Change Story

I'll end this chapter with my own story of how change has affected my career:

Most of the organizations of which I've been a working member have grappled with change. The magazine publishing firm where I held my first corporate job was threatened with a movement to unionize workers. To show its benevolence, presumably in the hope that employees would shun the union effort, the company initiated the rather peculiar practice of delivering a piece of fruit to workers every afternoon. After the company began firing those who were most vocal about unionizing, the fruit no longer tasted as sweet. I then worked as an editor at a startup magazine, where the constant struggle to stay afloat was the catalyst for organizational change. Eventually the owners lost the struggle and sold the magazine. The new owners moved it to another city, leaving the staff without jobs. Next stop was an ad agency, where winning and losing accounts drove constant change.

I then joined the staff of the independent newspaper that served a large university community. There, a new batch of student staffers arrived with each academic year, and elections of top editors regularly changed the face of newsroom management. From there I joined another newspaper in a highly competitive metropolitan market. The newsroom was constantly abuzz over the ambitious plans of our chief rival paper and how these plans prodded change at our paper. Suddenly, the competitor bought our paper with plans to merge it with its own newspaper. I moved on to the executive editorship of a group of weekly papers and soon learned that the first thing the publisher wanted me to do was fire the two highest-paid editors.

Leaving publishing to try public relations, I worked at a controversial reproductive-health organization that opened a new clinic, fought for continued government funding, and initiated testing for HIV and AIDS during my tenure. Next I became the speechwriter to an elected official, a position in which partisan politics spurred change. Nearly the last stop was a private university. Budget crises, enrollment challenges, and the drive for accreditation propelled change.

Overlapping my most recent jobs within organizations has been my effort to help people enter organizations, especially through written and spoken communication. As I have looked back at all the changing organizations I've been part of, I have to ask myself what I've learned. What have I discovered about driving, communicating, and coping with change that could help others? What could I have done differently to capitalize on organizational change? In what ways was I successful and proactive in encountering organizational change? What can my story and the telling of it communicate? How might I use my story to advance my career and guide others in employing story to advance their careers?

I then think about the career-management communication tools I have helped job seekers prepare for a number of years. This book has been the realization of my contention that storytelling should be part of networking, resumes, cover letters, job interviews, portfolios, and personal branding. These story elements can influence hiring managers. Most important, continued storytelling helps advance your career once you are on the job.

Summary

Storytelling is just as important on the job as it is to get the job. The ability to use stories to inspire and communicate about organizational change is especially critical in our turbulent global workplace. Just as you would seek to impress a prospective employer by telling stories about your accomplishments, you can stay on your current employer's radar by sharing the narrative of your achievements.

EPILOGUE

Let Your Career Story Unfold

My goal in this book has been to examine career stories to discover how they can apply to your efforts to enter organizations and to interact with these organizations in a fruitful way upon gaining entry.

Through detailed descriptions and many sample stories, I hope you've discovered the promise of incorporating tales of career accomplishment, especially your successful interaction with organizational change, into powerful communication that influences hiring managers. The evidence is clear that storytelling then propels your career by also enabling you to promote yourself, lead and communicate change, and interact successfully with change in your new workplace.

I hope you've begun to compose stories about yourself as you've read the book. Now is the time to take charge of your story and let your career story unfold.

I invite readers to contact me to share stories and ask questions about storytelling and careers. E-mail me at kathy@astoriedcareer.com. Please also visit my blog, http://astoriedcareer.com and the Career Storytelling section of Quintessential Careers: www.quintcareers.com/career_storytelling/.

Storytelling Resources

Following are resources for further information on the concepts introduced in each chapter.

Quintessential "You" Story Resources (Chapter 1)

Denning, S. (2005). *The Leader's Guide to Storytelling.* San Francisco, CA: Jossey-Bass.

Lambert, J. *Digital Storytelling Cookbook,* www.storycenter.org/cookbook.pdf.

Marshall, C., and Marshall, D. (1997). *The Book of Myself: A Do-it-Yourself Autobiography in 201 Questions.* New York, NY: Hyperion.

Simmons, A. (2006). *The Story Factor: Inspiration, Influence, and Persuasion through Storytelling.* Cambridge, MA: Basic Books.

Simmons, A. (2007). *Whoever Tells the Best Story Wins.* New York, NY: AMACOM.

Story-Development Resources (Chapter 2)

Atkinson, C.: Free story-building templates and resources, as described in the book, *Beyond Bullet Points* (although the book is about PowerPoint presentations, the templates and resources can be useful for any kind of story-building): www.sociablemedia.com/thebook_resources.php4.

Bolles, R. N. (2009 and annually). *What Color Is Your Parachute? 2009: A Practical Manual for Job-Hunters and Career Changers.* Berkeley, CA: Ten Speed Press.

Bronson, P. (2002). *What Should I Do with My Life?* New York, NY: Alfred A. Knopf.

Denning, S. (2001). *The Springboard.* Burlington, MA: Butterworth-Heinemann.

Denning, S. (2004). *Squirrel Inc.: A Fable of Leadership through Storytelling.* San Francisco, CA: Jossey-Bass.

Denning, S. (2005). *The Leader's Guide to Storytelling.* San Francisco, CA: Jossey-Bass.

Gargiulo, T. L. (2006). *Stories at Work.* Westport, CT: Praeger.

Han, P. (2005). *Nobodies to Somebodies: How 100 Great Careers Got Their Start.* New York, NY: Portfolio.

Maguire, J. (1998). *The Power of Personal Storytelling.* New York, NY: Tarcher/Putnam.

Neuhauser, P. C. (1993). *Corporate Legends & Lore: The Power of Storytelling as a Management Tool.* Austin, TX: PCN Associates.

Simmons, A. (2006). *The Story Factor: Inspiration, Influence, and Persuasion through Storytelling.* Cambridge, MA: Basic Books.

Simmons, A. (2007). *Whoever Tells the Best Story Wins.* New York, NY: AMACOM.

Sullivan, Rob (2001). *Getting Your Foot in the Door When You Don't Have a Leg to Stand On.* New York, NY: McGraw-Hill.

Sullivan, Rob. Story Sparking Blog: www.storysparking.blogspot.com.

Whitcomb, S. B. (2006). *Résumé Magic.* Indianapolis, IN: JIST Publishing.

Networking Resources (Chapter 3)

Bolles, R. N. (2009 and annually). *What Color Is Your Parachute?* Berkeley, CA: Ten Speed Press.

Enelow, W., and Goldman, S. (2005). *Insider's Guide to Finding a Job.* Indianapolis, IN: JIST Publishing.

Hansen, K. (2008). *A Foot in the Door: Networking Your Way into the Hidden Job Market*, Second Edition. Berkeley, CA: Ten Speed Press.

Quintessential Careers: "The Art of Career and Job-Search Networking": www.quintcareers.com/networking.html.

Quintessential Careers: "Informational Interviewing Tutorial": www.quintcareers.com/informational_interviewing.htm.

Resume Story Resources (Chapter 4)

Enelow, W., and Goldman, S. (2005). *Insider's Guide to Finding a Job.* Indianapolis, IN: JIST Publishing.

Gladwell, M. (2005). *Blink! The Power of Thinking Without Thinking.* New York, NY: Little, Brown.

Kraft, C. (2004, Nov. 9). "Don't just tell what you did, tell how you did it!" *Gladiator* newsletter. www.thegladiator.info/articles/kraft-howyoudid.phtml.

Quintessential Careers: Resume and CV Resources for Job-Seekers: www.quintcareers.com/resres.html.

Ryan, L. (2005, Feb. 22). "Multi-story resume, higher profile." *BusinessWeek* Online: www.businessweek.com/careers/content/feb2005/ca20050222_5064_ca009.htm?campaign_id=rss_crers

Whitcomb, S. B. (2006). *Résumé Magic.* Indianapolis, IN: JIST Publishing.

Cover Letter Resources (Chapter 5)

Hansen, K. (1998). *Dynamic Cover Letters for New Graduates: How to Write a Dazzling Cover Letter That Will Get Your Resume Read, Get You an Interview, and Get You a Great First Job!* Berkeley, CA: Ten Speed Press.

Hansen, K., and Hansen, R. S., Ph.D. (2001). *Dynamic Cover Letters: How to Write the Letter that Gets You the Job,* Third Edition. Berkeley, CA: Ten Speed Press.

Matias, L. "When Cover Letters Get Personal." Crossroads Jobseeker News: www.jobskills.info/career/cover-letters-personal.htm.

Quintessential Careers: "Cover Letter Resources for Job-Seekers": www.quintcareers.com/covres.html.

Portfolio Resources (Chapter 6)

Barrett, H. C. "Electronic portfolios as digital stories of deep learning." http://electronicportfolios.org/digistory/epstory.html.

Nelles, R. (2001). *Proof of Performance: How to Build a Career Portfolio to Land a Great New Job.* Manassas Park, VA: Impact Publications.

Quintessential Careers: "Job References & Portfolio Services for Job-Seekers." www.quintcareers.com/job_reference_services.html.

Satterthwaite, F., and D'Orsi, G. (2003). *The Career Portfolio Workbook.* New York, NY: McGraw-Hill.

Wortmann, C. "Beyond Bits and Bullets: Turning Strategy into Action Through Stories." WisdomTools: http://wisdomtools.com/documents/Beyond_Bits_and_Bullets.pdf.

Interviewing Story Resources (Chapter 7)

Enelow, W., and Goldman, S. (2005). *Insider's Guide to Finding a Job.* Indianapolis, IN: JIST Publishing.

Martin, C. (2004). *Boost Your Interview I.Q.* New York, NY: McGraw-Hill.

Quintessential Careers: "Guide to Job Interviewing Resources": www.quintcareers.com/intvres.html.

Terwelp, W. J. (2005). "Strategy to Boost Your Credibility." Career Hub: http://careerhub.typepad.com/main/2006/04/case_studies_bo.html.

Washington, T. (2004). Chapter 5: "Master the Art of Story Telling." In *Interview Power.* Bellevue, WA: Mount Vernon Press.

Personal Branding Resources (Chapter 8)

Andrusia, D., and Haskins, R. (2000). *Brand Yourself: How to Create an Identity for a Brilliant Career.* New York, NY: Ballantine.

Arruda, W., and Dixson, K. (2007). *Career Distinction: Stand Out by Building Your Brand.* Hoboken, NJ: John Wiley & Sons.

Arruda, W., and Dixson, K. "Career Distinction Workbook": www.careerdistinction.com/workbook/.

Godin, S. (2005). *All Marketers Are Liars.* New York, NY: Penguin.

Hilicki, C. (2005). *May I Have Your Attention, Please? Build a Better Business by Telling Your True Story.* Hoboken, NJ: John Wiley & Sons.

Peters, T. (1999). *The Brand You 50 (Reinventing Work): Fifty Ways to Transform Yourself from an "Employee" into a Brand That Shouts Distinction, Commitment, and Passion!* New York, NY: Knopf.

Quintessential Careers: "Tools for Career Networking on the Internet": www.quintcareers.com/Internet_networking_sources.html.

On-the-Job Storytelling Resources (Chapter 9)

Brown, D. W. (2002). *Organization Smarts.* New York, NY: AMACOM.

Callahan, S. (2006, April 30). "How to Use Stories to Size Up a Situation." www.anecdote.com.au/papers/Narrative_to_size_up_situation.pdf.

Callahan, S., Rixon, A., and Schenk, M. (2005, December). "Avoiding Change Management Failure Using Business Narrative": www.anecdote.com.au/papers/AnecdoteWhitePaper5NarrativeChangeMgt.pdf.

Clark, E. (2004, June 22). "Storytelling for Leaders": www.marketingprofs.com/4/clark1.asp (free registration at MarketingProfs site required).

Denning, S. (2001). *The Springboard.* Burlington, MA: Butterworth-Heinemann.

Denning, S. (2004). *Squirrel Inc.: A Fable of Leadership through Storytelling.* San Francisco, CA: Jossey-Bass.

Denning, S. (2005). *The Leader's Guide to Storytelling.* San Francisco, CA: Jossey-Bass.

Denning, S. (2007). *The Secret Language of Leadership.* San Francisco, CA: Jossey-Bass.

Gargiulo, T. L. (2002). *Making Stories: A Practical Guide for Organizational Leaders and Human Resource Specialists.* Westport, CT: Quorum.

Gargiulo, T. L. (2005). *The Strategic Use of Stories in Organizational Communication and Learning.* Armonk, NY: M. E. Sharpe.

Gargiulo, T. L. (2006, January). "Tell Us a Story." *American Executive:* www.americanexecutive.com/content/view/5583/.

Gargiulo, T. L. (2006). *Stories at Work.* Westport, CT: Praeger.

Goman, C. K. (2005, August). "12 Questions for Change Communicators." *Link&Learn eNewsletter:* www.linkageinc.com/company/news_events/link_learn_enewsletter/archive/2005/08_05_12_questions_goman.aspx.

Goman, C. K. (2006, January 9). "What's changed about change management?" *Communtelligence Newsletter:* www.communitelligence.com/blps/blg_viewart.cfm?bid=1&artID=1.

Johnson, S. (2002). *Who Moved My Cheese?* New York, NY: Putnam.

Kahan, S. (2004). "Every Professional Has Stories to Tell": www.sethkahan.com/Resources_0ProflStories.html.

Kotter, J. (2006, April 12). "The Power of Stories." *Forbes:* www.forbes.com/2006/04/12/power-of-stories-oped-cx_jk_0412kotter_print.html.

Maguire, J. (1998). *The Power of Personal Storytelling.* New York, NY: Tarcher/Putnam.

McKay, H. (1998, June). "Using Story as Strategy: Interview with David Barry, Ph.D.": www.australianstorytelling.org.au/txt/dbarry.php.

Neuhauser, P. C. (1993). *Corporate Legends & Lore: The Power of Storytelling as a Management Tool.* Austin, TX: PCN Associates.

Peck, D. (2004, August 23). "Changing Your Story": www.leadershipunleashed.com/pdf/ChangingYourStory.pdf.

Pink, D. (2006). *A Whole New Mind: Why Right-Brainers Will Rule the Future.* New York, NY: Riverhead Books.

Quintessential Careers: "Real World Section": www.quintcareers.com/Real_World/. New graduates tell stories of the change from being a college student to being a worker and describe positives and negatives of their first jobs.

Richards, D. (2004). *The Art of Winning Commitment: 10 Ways Leaders Can Engage Minds, Hearts, and Spirits.* New York, NY: AMACOM.

Silverman, L. (2006). *Wake Me Up When the Data Is Over: How Organizations Use Stories to Achieve Results* (2006). San Francisco, CA: Jossey-Bass.

Silverman, L., and Wacker, M. B. (2004). *Stories Tell: 55 Ready-to-Use Stories to Make Training Stick.* New York, NY: John Wiley & Sons.

Simmons, A. (2006). *The Story Factor: Inspiration, Influence, and Persuasion through Storytelling.* Cambridge, MA: Basic Books.

INDEX

A

B

C

D

E

F

G

H

I

R

S

T–V

W–Z